To Colin Ber
With very -q
wishes
Sheila Macey
April 1989.

THE FULL CIRCLE

THE FULL CIRCLE

by

Sheila Macey

Regency Press (London & New York) Ltd.
125 High Holborn, London WC1V 6QA

ISBN 0 7212 0672 7

Printed and bound in Great Britain by
Buckland Press Ltd., Dover, Kent.

DEDICATION

To my wonderful husband, Bill—
without whose help it would not have been written.

Acknowledgements

Lyn and Peter, Berenise,
Muriel Trigger and
Anne Secker

PREFACE

This book is an honest insight into the fascinating world of the unknown.

It tells how two people became involved, developed their psychic gifts, the many humorous incidents and the drama over a period of twenty years. Each chapter, contains a step by step account of the incredible journey which was taken. Not accepting, without first critically analysing, every aspect of the spiritual world. Its findings and its personal thoughts are described without prejudice. Leaving the reader, like the author, to draw whatever conclusion into the life hereafter.

CHAPTER ONE

THE FORTUNE TELLER

I was sitting in the stock-room. It was the morning coffee break and I was wondering to myself how our young son was behaving, having left him with a kind neighbour, when I suddenly became aware of eager conversation around me. Hearing my name, I looked up. "You would come wouldn't you Sheila—you are a bit that way yourself—so you are sure to want to come?" "Come where?" I asked. "Why to have your fortune told. I know a lady who is supposed to be really good," said my keen colleague. "O.K." I said, "I'm game—see if you can book my husband a sitting too!" From this simple conversation in an old stock-room was the beginning of my husband's and my introduction into spiritualism. The year was 1959.

I remember that night so well, travelling towards Hornsey looking for the house where the clairvoyant lived and arriving there full of apprehension. After being invited into the little back room at the top of the narrow staircase, we found there were about half a dozen of us—of which five of us made up our own party. Suddenly the door opened and a middle-aged lady came in and asked who was next. We each looked at one another—it reminded me a bit of the dentist's waiting-room. I said nervously that I would be next. I was then directed along the landing to a door right opposite the stairs. I knocked, and a very pleasant voice invited me to enter. My first reaction was one of surprise. I don't know what I expected certainly not anything so ordinary and bright. I remember thinking at the time what pretty coloured curtains and how nice the furniture was—it being of modern design, quite the opposite of my imaginary picture of dark drapes and dim lighting. On the contrary, everything about the room was so beautiful and bright. Having accustomed myself to the interior of my surroundings, I focused my eyes on a very attractive lady who was sitting very comfortably on an armchair to the left of the fireplace. Her dress matched the room—very modern and up-to-date. She smiled at me and with her hand gestured me to sit down on the vacant chair opposite her. I sat very uncomfortably on the edge of the chair and I could feel the ridge of the upholstery against my legs. I wanted to stand up immediately, but stupidly thought that if I moved I would break any vibrations which may have been building around me. That was as far as my knowledge of these things went at that time. So sitting in a most undignified position, my very first reading began.

"Do you know what I am?" were the first words uttered. How stupid, I thought, but answered in a whisper, "Oh yes, of course." "That's fine, " answered the lady, "For I do like my clients to know that I am not a fortune-teller." In one wild moment of panic I wondered how I could make a quick getaway. What was she talking about? The girls had said at the shop that she told fortunes. My mind at that moment was full of all sorts of weird things, and I am sure that had she waved a magic wand I could have turned easily into a frog without any effort on her part. "I am a spiritualist medium," she confirmed, as if she had been right in the middle of my jumbled, confused thoughts and knew that I was a novice to these things. Well, she could have said anything, for I had never come across Spiritualism until that moment.

My vast knowledge of the subject was the hilarious movie *Blythe Spirit,* but the thought that I was actually sitting with a real live medium, a concept which had not existed outside my imagination, gave me a feeling of awe and wonder. This lady didn't look a bit like the betrayal of the eccentric Madame Arcarti. What did amaze me was her down to earth and very ordinary natural attitude, and so, having nodded to her explanation, she proceeded to make communication with her spirit contacts. This so fascinated me, as I gazed at her, that she was able to have a conversation with unseen forms, I found it to be absolutely incredible. By this time I was enthralled. This medium was actually describing things about my personal life—accurate facts, which were so near to the truth. I listened intently and all too soon I came out of my fantasy world, hearing the words "Have you any questions to ask?" This took me completely unaware. I seemed to be in a trance and not one thing could my brain register—so I stumbled a few words which seemed, at the time, to be unintelligible, and so left the room.

I found my way back, hearing the excited chatter of those still waiting. Pulling myself together, I joined my friends, suddenly becoming aware of a very sore leg, and on looking down, noticed that the chair I had been sitting on had left an imprint on the skin. "Right," I said in a light-hearted voice, concealing hopefully my inner feelings which were of excited wonder, "Who's next?" I found myself a seat next to Bill, my husband. I could see he was in no hurry to take his turn and was giving the impression of gentlemanly behaviour—having decided definitely that he was going to be last. By that time I hoped his courage would last out—I knew him oh, so well! "That's perfectly O.K." he kept saying, "I don't mind, you go ahead." My friends looked gratefully at Bill, very impressed by his gallantry. They in turn, each had their sittings. I took note that they did not seem as excited as I was when they returned. They were laughing a great deal about what had been said—this seemed to agitate me somewhat. I didn't know why. I was just longing for Bill's turn to come so that we could go home and together discuss our night's adventure in the quiet of our then rather dingy old downstairs flat. Well I needn't have worried for I noticed as Bill came back into the room that he seemed rather flustered and by his manner I knew that he wanted to get away, and apart from an occasional nod here and there, that was the limit of his conversation until we arrived home.

"You put the kettle on dear, while I check the children are all right"—although I could tell by the silence that they were fast asleep. I called out to my friend, who lived upstairs, that we were home. I went down the four stairs which led into our tiny kitchen. I hated this place—everywhere was so dark. At that time I had not the slightest inclination to do anything about the dingy place, I'm afraid. To be perfectly honest, household chores were not one of my better talents. Had the surroundings been brighter perhaps the state of the flat would also have been better. The flat brings back to me many unbelievable thoughts that I could have actually lived amongst such a muddle of untidiness. I shudder now at the thought.

I slung off my shoes and moved a couple of items of clothing from the old armchair and sat down heavily. Bill looked oddly at me with an expression of a world within himself, to which I have since become very used to. "Well, what did you think?" he said. "Not quite what I thought it would be," I answered. He nodded, turning the gas-tap down as the water from the kettle boiled over. I watched him rinse under the tap a couple of cups he had taken out of the bowl which still held the evening's used utensils. "Do you think there's something in it?" he said, spooning the instant coffee into the cups, "I must admit she seemed really sincere, but I can't believe all of it—probably a lot of nonsense." He replaced the kettle and handed me the steaming coffee. "What did she say to you, Bill?" I said. "Oh, I can't remember a lot of it, but she was wrong about my job." "What about your job?" I said, looking at him intently. "Well, she said within three months I shall leave my job." "You must have got it wrong," I replied, knowing full well that it would take a miracle to move my husband from his work—that was something which was so predictable with him, change was not his line of country, being a very staid, quiet, sort of man. He was not one for moves, he had up until that time been in only two jobs since leaving school. The first one was in the optical trade, to which he returned after doing his National Service, and in which he was employed when we were first married. The second was in the printing trade. His father had been able to get him into this trade nine years previously. "Oh well," I said thoughtfully, "I suppose it could be true," knowing full well it would take a bomb to shift my Bill. Ambition was not his forté.

We both went to bed that night deep in thought. We had an odd conversation about the subject, but then dismissed it and continued our life, such as it was. I used to reflect back on the sitting quite frequently, and every time I did so, it seemed to put some sort of charge through me. However, as Bill obviously decided to forget the whole business, I kept these thoughts to myself.

It was six weeks after our visit to that medium, on a Friday evening which I shall never forget, that Bill opened the kitchen door and looked across at me and said, "That's it, it's happened." I was, as usual, sitting down in that dreadful room, litter everywhere, the children playing havoc with each other—the noise was awful. Our young son was airing his lungs, demanding attention for his food, and our little daughter was banging on the table with a metal spoon, making music, so she informed me.

"What has?" said I, completely uninterested. In those days I had become pretty bored with the same old routine, working at the shop, coming home each evening, never going anywhere. Visitors were not part of our little scene. Bill wasn't one for socializing and anyway the way in which I ran our home did not exactly create the right atmosphere to encourage guests. Bill must have been some sort of saint to have put up with my badly disorganized ways.

"I've been given the sack." I was just lighting a match and remember breaking it so I was left holding a minute piece on which the flame burned steadily. Amongst the noise I said in a cool voice, "Do you mind repeating that." "That's right," said Bill, "Watch it, you will burn your fingers. I've got the sack." I laughed, sort of, for I knew what had just been said was truly correct. Bill was not one for making up jokes. I digested the news carefully. "The sack, no Bill, it can't be, why you?" "Someone had to be used as an example and because of my continued lateness—well that's it." I might add, to be fair to his firm, it was justified. To a degree owing to the many hours of the day and night Bill had to work to bring in a little extra, he would sometimes come home from a night shift at about 5 a.m. and report for the day shift two hours later. This was at least twice a week—the poor man was exhausted. But after nine years, it seemed unbelievable, and moreover that the medium's words should come true so soon after our visit to her.

Once the initial shock had taken effect, we discussed long into the night the uncanniness of it. How on earth could she have known, we said, over and over again. As predicted the event had materialized. We waited until my husband had settled into a new job which took him some weeks. Eventually things calmed down and we were ready, this time on our own, to revisit this incredible lady, for that is how we felt about her. Having telephoned for an appointment, for which we had to wait some weeks, each of us felt an excitement within. In those early days we talked so much together which, in itself, was a wonder. For although our marriage was good it had got into a rut—like so many other couples' marriages seem to do. After the children had arrived we had, at that time, nothing in common, and it seemed now, looking back, that although we were together we were really apart. We never seemed to do anything, apart from work, and that to me was the limit of our conversation. So as the evening drew near for our appointment we had, within those short weeks of waiting, become very close.

Hand-in-hand we approached the house—looking at it as though it was some sort of magnificent castle and held a magic Merlin within. We were escorted into the now familiar back waiting-room. There was an old lady sitting by the window, her head touching the closed curtains. She had a serene look about her as she relaxed back against the upright chair. Her eyes were closed, but she seemed to be nodding to herself and smiling every now and then. I nudged Bill, who was sitting in the same chair as before, and he squeezed my hand. "I wonder what she will say this time," I whispered to him, and nervously giggled. At that moment the old lady looked strangely at us and spoke, not realizing that her few words were going to make history to two ordinary hard-up individuals. "Don't laugh at what you are told, remember all, for what is said will happen—Spirit does not lie." I nodded at her in agreement, not because I understood, but I knew from our recent happenings that I needed very little convincing of this medium's power. I heard footsteps coming towards the room. The old lady stood up, smiled at us both, and said, "You're next, my dears."

I felt my heart pulsating quickly, that strange feeling of excited panic came back to me. "Go on," said Bill. Once again I trod along that dark landing, fixing my eyes on the door. I knocked gently. Immediately, I recognised her kindly voice, as she bade me to enter. Nothing had changed within the room—still so lovely, bright and warm. "I've seen you before, have I not?" she said. She poked the coals which were stacked on the open grate, sending out spirals of winding smoke, which disappeared up the chimney. The fire suddenly, as if by magic, became alight with bright yellow and red flames, leaving their reflection on the brass coal scuttle, giving an impression of a dance. I looked at her attractive frame of build, very slim, I knew I was very badly out of proportion due to my lack of self-discipline—lumps of ugly fat protruding around my waist and stomach. I never did pay much attention when childbearing to keeping in shape. It seemed such a waste of time. My belief was that as you were going to grow fat anyway and would be eating for two, why not indulge in all sorts of fattening foods that were available.

Her hair was very dark, all but shoulder length, and she was wearing a very pretty pure white blouse and brown skirt. I felt very shabby standing there—my old plaid coat, well past its usefulness. Why hadn't I sewn on that button, I thought, as I put my hand across the offending opening. How old was she? I pondered—difficult to guess, I should say around her late forties. She invited me to sit down. This time I made sure I sat back comfortably. I quickly pulled my coat over my knees, as I saw a large, ugly ladder on one of my stockings, standing out proudly for all the world to see. Until now, I had never really taken much notice of my personal appearance, but here I was very conscious of my untidy dress and lack of fashion.

She proceeded as before, only this time I felt much more mentally equipped, and I was able to answer her when required. I became very absorbed, listening to her every word. "You will address people on a platform, many will listen," she said. "You have psychic gifts within which spirit will use—rare and beautiful together, yes together," she repeated. "Your husband will be with you, so many paths will you travel on your search for the truth. You have now entered into a complete change within your everyday way of life, you will find that not only will your thinking change, people will want to be near you. You find this difficult to comprehend," she said, "Spirit realizes your failings, they will help, do not fear, you have entered the first quarter of a circle, time and new faces in the material world will play an important part of your life."

Most of this sitting seemed so full of wonderful spiritual things that were to happen ahead. Although my understanding was still very much confused, I knew, somehow, that from then on I was going to investigate this so called Spirit world. I became aware then, and only then, that what was around me as a child must link together somewhere. "Now let me see your husband," she said. I stood up, not wishing to leave this tiny sanctuary of safety, which is how I felt about it. To me, that little room meant being in someway in a dream world, a fairy story where all dreams come true. Reluctantly, I left, and made my way back across the landing towards my husband who was waiting. He stood up as soon as I entered, this time very eager for his turn. He smiled nervously, and was gone.

I sat down in the same chair that the old lady had occupied

earlier, and lent back in the same fashion as she had done, feeling my hair touch the curtains. I closed my eyes—there was no one else around to watch me. I was alone. I reflected back to the words which had been spoken to me. Oh Sheila, I thought, it's ridiculous. How on earth could you be addressing people—just look at you, be realistic. We live in an old flat, not only small and badly in need of repair, and we never have anyone come to see us now—so how come all that is going to change suddenly. Who is going to produce suddenly, many people, who would want us for ourselves? No, it just didn't make sense. Perhaps Bill's reading would be more constructive for us to get some sort of lead, where to start, if indeed this was to be our future.

Bill was ages. I thought he was never coming out. I heard his voice at last and also the medium's. They were laughing together. I heard him thank her and then the door closed and Bill's footsteps could be heard coming across the landing. I stood as he entered the room. "Let's get back home," I said, "I've got so much to tell you." "So have I," said Bill, tucking his arm around what looked like a couple of newspapers, although I knew for a fact that he had not brought them with him. We climbed down the stairs, where I suppose the medium's husband was waiting, for a man was waiting at the bottom to let us out. We exchanged a pleasant few words and then left. To my memory that was the last time we went to that house in Hornsey. I didn't know then, but my husband had under his arm the ammunition which gave us the first step into our long search ahead.

We were both pretty silent on the drive home. Like before, we savoured what we each had to say, to be analyzed in the privacy of our own home, as if unseen forms would interfere or interrupt our full minds. Arriving home, after checking all was well with the children, I quickly ran down the stairs into the kitchen, banging the door with my heavy frame. It was a solid door, but because of the ball-catch could be very easily opened with a gentle push. I couldn't, at the best of times, open the door quietly, and was always inclined to be a bit heavy-handed. This night it seemed to make an unearthly crash and Bill looked with annoyance at me, but didn't say anything. I lit a cigarette, took the cup of coffee which Bill had prepared, and sat down, automatically throwing off my shoes as I did so. I looked thoughtfully at him. He seemed to be trying to talk to me, but was finding the words difficult. He repeated the word, "Well," at least three times. "Go on," I said encouragingly, "You speak first." "What do you know about healing?" he said, in a very quickened voice. "I don't, why?" I said. "Well, I'm supposed to have the power." My husband was looking at me very seriously. "One day I shall cure all sorts of complaints, she also mentioned cancer. Oh, and you and I will work together on some sort of platform preaching to others. Are we going mad, love?" He said.

As I watched his eyes looking around our very poor, very untidy kitchen, for one mad moment I wanted, there and then, to spring-clean everything within that awful room, but giving thought to using all that energy and the amount of work it would entail, quickly I dismissed it from my mind. "Yes, she told me similar things," I said. "What does it all mean, Bill? Why us? What's so special about us?" I repeated. "If she came home and saw this mess and knew about all the debts we have she would soon change her mind," I said, feeling at that moment very sorry for myself. But it was true, we didn't have two half-pennies for a penny—we were in debt up to our eyebrows. This fact was possibly due to our very speedy marriage. At the very young age of seventeen years, and Bill just two years older, we had decided upon an early marriage, due to my pregnancy. In fact, Bill and I met and were married within four months of meeting each other, and although this had happened a few years earlier, we had never been able to pick ourselves up, so to speak—mainly, I think, because of my total inadequacy to keep house. I was an absolute dreamer and couldn't manage the responsibility of household management and was for ever getting into all sorts of trouble where money was concerned.

"Maybe we gave her the wrong impression of us," I said, "Or at least me," I hastily added as Bill looked quickly at me. "I just can't see myself preaching anyway—I don't know much about religion, I could never understand the bible at school, it never did make sense. Well, that's what she said," I answered Bill before he even asked the question. "She said preach and in my book that means the bible, and that's out for me," I now said raising my voice heatedly. "Maybe it's not that at all." said Bill. "Look, she gave me these newspapers to read." "Oh, I wondered why you had them," I replied, as I picked one up from the table. *The Psychic News*—I opened the pages carefully. "She told me to look at the back for a list of spiritualist churches—should be one in most areas," Bill said, looking at the other paper. "Ah, here we are, gosh there's a lot all over the place. I didn't realize there were so many. Why there's one just at the top in Stonebridge Road." "Where's that?" I said. Although I was living in North Tottenham we had not been there very long having moved from Edmonton just a couple of years previously—therefore, Tottenham was not that familiar to me, but Bill was born and bred in the area so knew most parts. "It's not far from here—wouldn't take more than ten minutes to get there," Bill's voice was sounding very keen, "They have some sort of service on Sunday evenings at 6.30 p.m. Let's go, it could be interesting—maybe we'll get some kind of lead as to what it's all about." "Oh, I don't know," I said, feeling a little scared.

Had I made the suggestion I wouldn't have cared a damn, because that was me. If I made a decision, right or wrong, which was many times, that was O.K. as far as I was concerned, but for my Bill to make the first move was, in itself to me, quite extraordinary, and this worried me. "When?" I said to him. "Why not this Sunday? The children should be all right. I expect upstairs," he said, looking towards the ceiling, "will keep an eye." "She'd collapse if I told her where we were going, I can just see her now taking the micky. 'Going to church? Sheila, oh, how nice!'" I started copying our neighbour's mannerisms, which never failed to make Bill laugh. I always was a bit of a comedian. "Oh, stop it and be serious for a minute—there's no need to tell her where we're actually going. Just tell her we will be popping out for a while." I could see Bill wanted to get this settled here and now, for his voice carried some sort of urgency, as if he was being pushed to get things started. So I nodded in agreement. "O.K. let's go then," thinking to myself as I said it that we still had a few days to go. Hopefully, Bill might change his mind.

Church, I thought, when we went to bed that night, how boring! I could think of much better things to do rather than sit in some dreary old cold church. Then, as if answering myself, I thought, well, what do we do on Sundays? Nothing, simply nothing. We slept half the morning, had dinner late, and usually wasted the rest of the day looking at the old television set which invariably would play up and spoil whatever was on. "Perhaps we ought to leave it Bill," I whispered. No answer came from his still form beside me. I quickly pulled the sheet over my head. I had always been afraid of the dark and this night seemed very frightening to me. I kept thinking about the medium saying, "I see Spirit with you." She had repeated this to me more than once. Spirit, I thought, I wonder if they can see me.

I got closer to Bill, my arm around his waist. I could feel the warmth of his back and the gentle movement of his breathing as he was in the world of sleep. My husband a healer—what a thought, why I can hardly get him to make conversation with any of my friends on the occasions he pops into the shop for me on Saturdays. He always shys away from them. Yet wouldn't it be lovely, I thought, going into a world of fantasy, seeing my Bill standing on a hillside, with arms outstretched, as all the people from down the street came towards him asking him to touch them! I smiled to myself, that would give old Mrs. Nosy Parker up the road something to think about. My dream world became more far-fetched as I pictured myself within a large cathedral, wearing a flowing gown of white, approaching a rostrum, smiling at the people as I went.

I shook myself, pull yourself together, I thought, as I crept further under the sheets. How could Bill sleep so easily with so much about to happen, I thought, but his steady breathing confirmed that he was indeed asleep. I felt so wide awake, my mind taking me back to my childhood—so many strange things used to happen to me then. I remembered the time I saw an old man looking at me through my mother's front-room window, and my screaming with fright, causing havoc, sending my father and brother to look for an imaginary man. At least, that's what I was led to believe even though I protested that he was really there. Many times I was scolded because of these different visitations which I was told were no more than my imagination. I wonder if this has something to do with my feelings when something had happened to Bill at his work—particularly when others around him were having some sort of problem or other. I could usually ask him what was up that day, although I mostly knew, but we always dismissed it as sixth sense—nothing more than that. But I was beginning to think now that maybe this could be linked together. I felt an excited thrill run through my body as I seemed to be unravelling some gigantic jigsaw puzzle. I didn't feel quite so badly about the approaching Sunday now—especially if it was going to open the secret doors of mystery.

I began to feel tiredness creeping over me. I yawned loudly, disturbing Bill as I did so, but just for a moment. Oh well, who knows, if this was to be the beginning of some great adventure, one thing was for sure, we had nothing to lose, our life as it is now is just an existence. Sunday we are going to church.

Sunday, I thought, Sunday.

CHAPTER TWO

THE CHURCH CIRCLE

We had dinner early. Things were going exceedingly well. The children seemed to be exceptionally good. My daughter was trying hard to please me and our young son was playing cars quietly on the back doorstep. I could hear the music from a radio playing in the distance—probably next door's, I thought. It gave me a feeling of tranquillity, if that's the word one could use. For this day was no different to any other Sunday except that we were on the verge of actually going to enter into something, I didn't know quite what. Deep down within me I had this feeling, of which I was very much aware, that life was about to open its mysterious doors, and a sort of thrill kept going on inside me. Because of this inner peace that I felt maybe the word "tranquillity" was not such an odd word.

I also found myself tidying up our little flat—that is, more than I usually did. Somehow I felt that if I was to go to church I ought to tidy up a little. Silly, when I look back, but I was so scared of maybe being found out that I kept an untidy household and that it might jeopardize our future pathway into spiritualism.

Wiping the table where our son had left some remnants of food, which would have been demolished had he seen it, I thoughtfully wondered, as I rinsed the dishcloth under the tap, whether our kids could do with a more reformed mother. I told myself they would, though not liking the thoughts I was having, but I knew it was true. I wasn't a bad mother, like going off and leaving them, or being over-spiteful in my chastisement of them, my problem was I just never seemed to care enough about the everyday normal family upbringing which goes with the responsibility of being a parent. I was too dreamlike, too unreliable, that was me. I needed a jolly good shake up. I felt uncomfortable. I wasn't too keen on the way my thoughts were going, clearly making me face the truth.

I continued busying myself, getting quite carried away, tidying up the clothes which were draped all over the armchair, putting them into a neat pile on the chair by the table. "Can I play out?" asked my daughter, disturbing my far-away thoughts. She was, until then, playfully trying to make a bridge out of empty cornflake cartons for our son's cars to go across. She had obviously got tired of being an engineer and was wanting to exert her energy on some other form of entertainment. "Well, don't go away from the front door," I said. That was all I needed if she was to go wandering off. This was sometimes her habit, giving us, on many occasions, all sorts of panic. "I promise, mummy," she said.

I was left alone with our little boy who was still sitting on the step, completely absorbed and trying, with great difficulty, to cross the make-do bridge of cardboard with a large heavy old wooden train which had seen better times, the paint being hardly recognizable. It still, however, brought great joy to its eager master and that made it well-worth the threepence I had paid for it down at the jumble sale the previous week. The cardboard bridge caved in due to its heavy load. "Try one of your other cars," I said to him, "That's much too heavy, son." But no, evidently he was going to continue his impossible feat. I left him, not wishing to cause any uproar on this rather unusually pleasant afternoon.

Bill wouldn't be long now. He sometimes popped over to see his dad on Sundays. Poor old dad, he seemed so lost since losing mum. I had quite liked my mother-in-law. During the short time I had known her she had always been so very kind to me although it must have been hard on her to lose her youngest son to somebody like me. I'm sure, had she been honest, she would have wanted someone far better than me for her son, although not for one minute did she give that impression when I broke the news of my pregnancy. Her words, I remember, were, "If Bill has done this to you then he must marry you, my dear—the arrangements must be made immediately." Such an honest, respectful lady. Had she lived longer I'm sure I could have grown to love her, but she was taken from us twelve months after our little girl was born. I recall how shattered Bill was and how he had cried. Poor Bill, he was only twenty-one when he lost her. It had shaken us all even though she had been very ill with cancer. She had survived an intricate operation and was recovering so well—we were all so proud of her remarkable will-power, when suddenly, without warning, whilst returning from holiday, she was taken ill and died on the train coming back to London. Such a cruel blow to bear. It took Bill weeks to accept her death. Being the youngest of six children he was very close to his mum.

So now he would often pop over to see his dad who didn't live very far away from us. I looked at the clock—it was still quite early. I finished tidying the flat, after a fashion, piling the dirty crocks in the sink. I'll wash up later, I thought, but something inside me said, no, do it now. I shrugged, trying to ignore this saintly being within me who was beginning to make a habit of changing my ways—this was annoying to say the least.

I picked up the kettle and filled it to overflowing simply because I had, in quick temper, turned the water tap on full. The water came rushing out like some sea serpent. I turned off the tap, drenching myself into the bargain, and tipped the excess water from the kettle. I then placed it with a firm bang on the gas stove. If only we had an Ascot, I thought, it would make life so much easier instead of having to boil a kettle every time we wanted hot water. I lit the gas, turning the tap on full, allowing the flames to escape from the bottom and lick the sides of the kettle, fascinating me. I'll wash up, but nothing more, I thought. This extra effort was becoming far too exhausting, I thought, and I really must try my best to look presentable tonight. I think I'll wear my green lurex suit, the one I wore for Bill's old firm's party—it's not very elegant, but at least with a press here and there it wouldn't look too bad!

I decided I had better check where it was. Knowing me it could be anywhere. I nipped into the bedroom, my eyes blind to the disarray before me, pulling the old wardrobe door open. I looked inside, smelling that old familiar smell which one seems to associate with old furniture, like mothballs, although I had never used them, probably the previous owner had. "Ah, here's the skirt," I said out loud, finding it crumpled up in the corner. Now for the jacket. I saw it hanging half-on and half-off the coat hanger. Bundling the two pieces together under my arm, I ran back downstairs, banging the bedroom door as I did so.

The kettle was now bubbling merrily and sending its lid noisily up and down, making sizzling sounds as the water was spurted out on to the red-hot burner. I turned off the tap, giving it a blinding look—just as if it had no right to be making such an awful fuss. My son had now discovered to his dismay, that the wooden engine was indeed far too heavy for the cardboard bridge and had neatly torn the offending article into two pieces. He disgustedly threw the offending parts on to the back step, letting me know into the bargain that he was not a bit amused. I concealed the temptation to say, I told you so, but gave him a biscuit instead. I picked up the biscuit tin I had managed to knock down whilst retrieving the electric iron from the same cupboard. I stood on the chair and fixed the bayonet plug into the light socket. I placed the iron carefully on its end and then waited, hands on hips, for it to heat up.

That's when Bill came in, carrying our daughter on his shoulders. "Watch out," I said, as she almost hit her head on the ceiling. "I want a go," said our son, demanding instant attention. Bill picked him up, now having the two children perched perilously on his shoulders. "Oh, do be careful," I said, as delighted screams came from both of them. I decided, at that moment, to wash up the dirty dishes, partly I suppose because I wanted Bill to notice my reformed ways, and partly because I knew he would be using the kettle to make coffee. He always made coffee on returning home from whence he had been. I poured the boiling water over the greasy dishes and watched as the hot water made shiny slithers of fat all around the bowl. Washing up liquid was a luxury which had never seen its way into my abode. The tea-towel was hanging on a little line above the sink. I pulled it down and proceeded to wipe the dishes. I was having terrible difficulty in not burning my fingers as I did so for I was carefully taking each plate out of the steaming water, one at a time, not letting them drain, which had the obvious outcome of making my tea-towel thoroughly wet.

Bill had put the children down and they had gone into the little back yard. They were excitedly opening "Jamboree Bags", which probably Bill's sister had sent them. "How's it going," he said, looking around, "Blow, you've been busy." He said no more, but I could read his thoughts when he saw the cleared table and the neat pile of clothes on the chair. To say he was surprised would be an understatement. Shocked, more like, I would say.

I picked up the the green suit from the table. "This what you're going to wear tonight?" Bill said. "What else have I got," I replied. "I never said anything, did I, you'll look fine in that once its had a bit of press." "Would you do me a favour and get me a blanket off one of the children's beds?" I asked. The table was my only means for ironing at that time. Whilst Bill went for the blanket, I clipped off an offending piece of hair which kept falling on to my face and going in my eyes. Having secured back my hair, I hastily pulled open the lid of a box which I kept on a shelf under the sink. Around this box was a thin silver chain which I hoped would keep the lid secure.

I searched amongst the assortment of bits and pieces, which was mostly rubbish, as I knew that I had seen some hair curlers there the last time I had had an occasion to look in the box. I turned over what seemed to be something very odd and felt peculiar in my hand, but found it was only a piece of old fur which had somehow managed to get very wet. I threw it into the fireplace with a "Ugh, nasty," speaking to myself. Ah, there they are. I pulled out a paper bag triumphantly. It was always a miracle when something was found. Turning the curlers out of the bag I then quickly proceeded to roll up tightly my over-bleached hair, taking note that the iron by this time had become very, very hot. I turned off the switch. Better not scorch my suit or I shall be in trouble I thought.

Bill, by this time had returned with the blanket and was telling me about his sister and what had been happening to her and how his dad was. I tried to show some sort of interest, answering him here and there with an odd "Yes," or "Mmm," when required. I spat on the iron—it sizzled, better leave it for a few more minutes. I continued curling my hair. That should do it, I thought, as I twirled the last bit of hair on to my last curler.

I felt the iron once again, having assured myself, by its feel, that I was not about to burn the lurex. I pressed the skirt, noting that a stitch was required on the hem. I would do that in a minute. The jacket didn't need much pressing—once I'd done the sleeves where the coat-hanger had left an out-of-shape mark on the shoulders. "There," I said to Bill, "That's not too bad." "Take the plug out, will you," I asked, as I lay the now tidy-looking suit on the back of the armchair. "You had better get the kids some tea, love, before we go out. We don't want old moaner," said Bill, indicating with an upward movement of his eyes, "Our upstairs neighbour, saying that the kids are hungry and she had to feed them, do we." "All right, give me a minute, I've only just washed up and I haven't stopped since dinner," I said hotly. "Look, I'll do them some toast after I've had a cuppa and a cigarette, O.K." I said in a threatening voice, which meant "Don't push me or else," meaning it wouldn't take me long to change my mind about the evening.

Bill didn't say another word, taking himself outside to the yard where the children were playing, chasing them. Once again shrieks of excitement were coming from them as Bill fooled about. He loved playing with the children and didn't appear to hear the noise that they made. For the onlooker it was bedlam. After a while I saw to the children's tea, washed their faces and tidied them in a general way. I deposited them upstairs with my neighbour, ignoring their protests. My neighbour greeted me at the gate, which was at the top of the stairs put there to stop the escape of her young toddler. She quickly took my two from me and, as I retraced my steps down the stairs, I called back to her that we wouldn't be out long and hoped to return home early. Of course I didn't know how long we would be gone, but not giving one hint as to where we were really going, I prayed it would not take long.

It took me just about five minutes to get ready, having prepared myself earlier. I brushed my hair and tried to make it into some kind of style. Now that it was curled, my ugly black roots showed through the bleach, which didn't help. Still, I was quite pleased with the final result and looked at my reflection approvingly. Bill was ready, looking as always clean and tidy. Personal hygiene had always been most important to my husband and no matter what else happened, a strict washing routine was always part of his day before retiring to bed.

"How do I look," I said, turning round doing a model's pose. "Fine," he said, "Are you ready. It's nearly six-o'clock—we had better not be late, I'm not exactly sure where it is." "Right then, let's go." I slipped my feet into my one-and-only pair of shoes, which incidentally didn't match my suit, and away we went. I got into our car, making myself comfortable. I noticed old Nosy Parker looking through her lace curtains. I always had a strong inclination, and especially at that moment, to poke my tongue out at her, but decided against this childish whim. She always annoyed me and was probably taking note of the fact that the kids were not with us and that we must therefore be off to somewhere special and not just out for an early evening drive.

We were lucky to have the car—the only bit of luxury we allowed ourselves. Bill was making sure we would keep up the payments for he paid them weekly himself, not daring to give me a smell of the money for fear of having the care repossessed. The car started first time, as usual. I looked at Bill. I knew just how proud he was of the way he kept it immaculate—like some shiny white chariot—a complete contrast to the havoc of his home.

"Here we are," said Bill. I could see a very old-looking orthodox church. As we pulled up a little past the door, Bill switched off the engine. We just sat there—neither of us keen to make the first move. "It's only ten past six now, let's have a cigarette," I said, pulling Bill's shirt cuff back over his wrist so that I could look at his watch. "Good idea," said Bill. I watched as my husband rolled his cigarette, carefully tucking the tobacco into the fine paper, pinching off the ends and putting the tiny scraps of tobacco back into his pouch. I saw one or two people going into the church. I wonder how many are inside, I pondered, not many I should think, there doesn't seem to be much activity going on. Bill nudged me. "Ready, it's twenty past, better go in now." I nodded and got slowly out of the car taking as much time as I could.

I was feeling very strange—that same feeling which I had become quite accustomed to. I could feel my heart beating rapidly. I knew by Bill's vacant look that he was experiencing something similar. We approached the door and nervously entered. An elderly priest, known as Brother John, welcomed us with a warm handshake. I could feel the strength of his hands and yet he looked very old and frail. I then became aware of our surroundings, noting first the smell. Churches, to me, always did smell. Not unpleasant, but a different aroma peculiar to them. Even now, I can still detect that same smell when entering a church, whether the building be old or new, and still find myself sniffing the hymn books as if they might give some hint as to its hidden whereabouts.

We settled down on the very back pew, hoping that we would be inconspicuous. I did note that the people were laughing and exchanging pleasantries with one another, not as had been the custom with my upbringing, together with many others, that silence in church was a must and an order to be obeyed. Bill and I didn't speak, but busily took in the scene, listening to other people's conversation, trying to catch what they were saying without giving the impression of eavesdropping. I must admit, from what I heard out of the speaker in front of us, it sounded a lot of rubbish, completely way out, I thought.

Oh, how I've come across these people since then—so bad for our movement, making out Spirit to be so terribly weird. Even then I remember thinking they must be nut cases. I gave Bill an odd sort of look knowing full well he was thinking the same as me. I managed to ignore their voices and concentrated on the proceedings, having watched a lady going on to the rostrum and, to my great surprise, a man dressed in the clothes of a bishop. I was to learn, within minutes of the opening service, that we were indeed being honoured by the Bishop of Hastings, who was to address us on this special day, it being Palm Sunday.

After an introduction of welcome we commenced the singing of the opening hymn, which I seemed to recognise having sung it at Sunday School. I'm afraid that apart from the voices from the platform the singing sounded pretty weak, but we battled through four verses, and as the last line was coming to a close I sighed with relief. We sat down and the bishop led us into prayer. I don't exactly know my feelings at that time. I can remember feeling safe, seeing the cross on the altar, which strangely made me feel protected, and yet I was not, at that particular time, very religious. Somehow, looking at that cross placed in the centre of the altar, with flowers either side, it gave me a great sense of security.

The man, known as Brother John, spoke to us all—looking down upon the tiny congregation he spoke of his great thrill that the Bishop of Hastings had willingly come to serve us and of how deeply honoured he was to welcome him. He also introduced us to the medium, who was he said, warmly welcomed in his church, her name being Vera Amsdon. We sang another hymn and then the Bishop of Hastings addressed us. To be honest I really cannot remember what was said, but it was obviously to do with the day being Palm Sunday. I felt no feeling of attraction towards the service and this experience was to me just as boring as church had always been. This could possibly have been that as an evacuee I was forced to attend church three times every Sunday.

I began to fidget, boredom setting in. The bishop's voice continued on and on—yet, although it seemed uncanny, I could feel his eyes upon me, drawing me, as if by some magnetic force, towards him. To my relief he then drew his speech to a close. I breathed heavily, glad to be released from the tension, feeling my body relax, as the chairman asked us to sing the now familiar hymn of *Open Thine Eyes,* that we may prepare the pathway for our Spirit friends to join us.

I looked around the church quickly and felt instinctively, yet again, this strange thrill within. As the last few words were sung I noticed the lady, who presumably was the medium, making her way towards the front of the rostrum singing with us as she made her approach. She stood patiently as the organist played the last strains "Amen".

Things then changed dramatically. I found myself very alert, fascinated and spellbound, as she proceeded, at random to pick out different members of the congregation, going from one side of the church to the other. From the answers she was receiving it was evident that her spiritual contacts were indeed, making through her, very accurate communications. She was telling a lady, who was sitting near the front, that Spirit was very encouraged by her fine progression and was proud of her efforts, when suddenly she broke away and said, "I want to speak to the gentleman sitting in the back row." I felt Bill's body slowly sinking down within his seat. "You, sir," she said, looking straight at Bill. "Come on now, let me hear your voice, don't be afraid, that's better," she approved. Bill spoke a quiet, "Do you mean me?"

She then described an old gentleman to him, with a shock of white hair, tall, heavy build, she went on. Bill said he wasn't sure who the spirit was. "Never mind," she said, "Go to your relatives and ask them—they will give you the confirmation of who has visited you this night." She stopped speaking at this point, but seemed to be listening to someone else, when she nodded as if showing that she understood. She then addressed Bill again. "You are seeking, doors are opening for you, but you will not find it here. Look around, you must reach out, seek further and help will be forthcoming. I wish you luck." She smiled at Bill as if seeing him brought back memories of her own quest for knowledge. "Don't give up, dear," she said motherly to him, smiling also at me, and dismissed the conversation abruptly.

What went on afterwards I really cannot recall. More hymns were sung and both the Bishop and Brother John spoke again—and then it was over. Bill and I quickly got up from our seats and made our way along the pews to the entrance where we had come in. The Bishop was standing at the door, exchanging words as the people began to leave. As we, in turn, came up to him, he gave us both a cross made of palm leaves which I have, to this day, kept as a memory, not only of the meeting being our first at a Spiritualist church, but also it serves as a reminder of kind thoughts to the memory of Vera Amsdon, who died a few years later. Vera Amsdon was the second link to our very long chain of investigation.

On returning home that night, silence yet again prevailed, as if one word would break the magic spell, each within our thoughts not yet ready to be uttered until we could, as before, be hidden behind closed doors. One thing was for sure, we would accept the advice given and not return to that particular church for we both felt no inner feeling of enthusiasm or pulling force to return—this we decided on reaching home, making certain that we were indeed alone. We spoke long into the night, each expressing views on our feelings. Was spiritualism gaining a hold on us? Hard to say at that time, for we were still so new to the experience. It had certainly awakened something within us, but as before, we remained, feet firmly on the ground, not allowing ourselves to become too involved. We decided to leave it awhile and maybe seek further should we feel the need to do so.

Life returned as before—each week the same as the last—neither of us mentioning our recent visit to the church, until that is, we were at Bill's dads and his elder sister was there. Suddenly, without warning, Bill started asking her all sorts of questions on their distant relatives. I heard her describing the self-same gentleman that Vera Amsdon had described. It was apparently their great-grandfather. I joined in the conversation and explained the nature of our enquiry. Bill's sister listened intently, showing interest, and by the way her eyebrows raised, I knew she was enjoying the limelight in being able to reveal the history of the Macey ancestry. Yes, without a doubt, we had found the Spirit who had shown himself and had allowed himself to be recognized through the eyes of the medium, now duly identified as being a great-grandfather to Bill.

Once again, on returning home, we found ourselves searching

the paper which held the list of spiritualist churches. The *Psychic News* was indeed finding its use, as I am sure to many others on their first enquiries into the unknown. "We can always travel to Wood Green," said Bill, "That's not far away, I see they have services twice a week, Wednesdays and Sundays—we could give it a try." "Yes, we must," I said, "I really want to know more." I watched Bill's eager face searching the many listed churches, his finger running up and down the lists. "Seems to me," he said, "That Wood Green is about the nearest, apart from the one we've already been to. Let's go, if we make it on Wednesday we can leave the children in bed and won't have to answer any awkward questions, just ask if upstairs will keep an eye on them. She'll think we're popping out to the pictures or something like that—much easier than explaining an early outing on a Sunday." "Yes, you're right," I said, already feeling the excitement building up in me, "What we could do is go for a ride round and find out where this church is and then we'll be able to go right to it on Wednesday night."

So this we did. We were impressed by the outside appearance of the church, which was a very smart-looking corner house—the entrance was around the side and looked like an ordinary back gate. On being sure that this was the church of our intention we returned home and waited patiently for the Wednesday evening to come. Eventually it did and, as before, I found things at home going like clockwork, the children being perfect angels and were already for bed when Bill came home from work. As usual, the temptation to fool around with them could not be resisted and for ten minutes or so the kitchen was like a tornado—things being knocked over as the children were flung, with delighted glee, up and over Bill's shoulders. Shouts of "More dad, I want more daddy." How they never got hurt I shall never know. To an outsider you would have thought they were being murdered. Peace, at last, was restored, as Bill sharply spoke "Enough," and sat down to eat his dinner.

Then, as before, I noticed Bill's approval as he saw I had, in a fashion, made an effort to bring some sort of tidy order into the small room. He quickly picked up a couple of items of laundry that had fallen to the floor when caught by the feet of flying legs, of which Bill had been the instigator. "I see you've been busy," he said, as he tucked in to the minced meat and potatoes. I nodded, pleased that my hard efforts had been noticed. I watched Bill as he ploughed his way through his meal, using his fork to mash the potatoes, until his dinner looked like one ugly mess. This irritated me, although Bill mostly did this with anything on which gravy had been placed. I couldn't cook too well, but somehow I did like to make a meal look attractive.

Funny that, looking back over the years I had always had some sort of obsession about the appearance of food on a plate. To me, food tasted so much better if it was presented well. This was probably due to my being a bit of a glutton and therefore, if nothing else, food should be treated with the greatest respect. I could guarantee my husband's actions when minced meat was on the menu. Having mashed carefully all the potato with the minced meat he would then pick up a dessert spoon and begin to eat with great relish, not hurriedly, but enjoying each spoonful, taking it from the side of the plate, taking care not to burn his tongue on the hot food. "I shan't take long getting ready," he stated, as he finished the last mouthful. Bill always left a few mouthfuls for our little son, who was patiently waiting for his dad to finish, wolfing it down as if he hadn't eaten for days instead of about half-hour previously. "Come on now, children," I said, "Time for bed."

I was wanting to settle them early, for as always the first few minutes was spent on getting drinks of water or finding the particular cuddly toy which would be spending the night with its owner. As I was running back and forth, fetching this and that, I wondered why it was that children have a knack of demanding attention and knowing, particularly at bedtime, that their needs were carried out by their parents as if they were slaves obeying every order. They seemed to know that mummy and daddy were at their most vunerable at that time, possibly jealous because they knew they would not be included once bedtime separated them for us. At last they were settled and I went back into the kitchen.

Bill had just finished washing and so within half-an-hour we were leaving the house once again to go to another meeting, not quite so green as before. At least we have an idea of what's what, I thought, as the car started up. The journey took a while and I was glad to sit back on the seat and relax. It had been a long day, busy at the shop, and my feet were aching. I was just about to say to Bill how tired I was feeling, when he interrupted my thoughts. "This is where we shall stay," he said, as he signalled to the approaching traffic his intentions. "Stay, stay where?" I said, completely lost as to what he was talking about. "At this church, where we are going." "How do you know?" I said. "I don't, but I just feel it somehow," Bill's voice sounded a little odd. "Oh come off it, stop fooling about—we haven't even been inside the place yet, so how can you say that?" He shrugged his shoulders, keeping his eyes firmly on the road ahead.

I began to feel that odd strangeness again. We must be getting near, I thought, looking about me. I noticed the garage with its lights now shining like a beacon, illuminating the forecourt, where stood some very handsome-looking cars for sale. I knew that just past the garage we had to turn for that was our landmark. Bill expertly turned the car and we were there. I could see a few places where we could park, but left the decision to Bill, and found that we were going quite a little way past the church before the car was brought to a halt. "How's the time?" I asked. "Nearly twenty-past-seven, better not hang about—it's taken a bit longer than the other day, a lot more traffic about." I waited as Bill locked his door and, as usual, checked mine.

Together we walked into the side entrance which led us up to a little pathway in the garden of the house. I couldn't see too much although above the gate was a bright white light which lit up the gateway, but its power didn't do much more than that. I noticed ahead of me two doors open, probably french doors. We entered and immediately were greeted with a most friendly handshake from a lady who was standing just inside the entrance. Her smile was enchanting. "How nice to see you both," she said, as if knowing us as some long-lost acquaintances. I smiled back at her, thanking her for the welcome. Holding our hymn books we were escorted into a rather large room, which most definitely resembled a church. In fact, I would say it was a most beautiful room. I looked around, amazed. There were rows upon rows of chairs with many people filling them, the empty seats quickly being taken. I noticed, above all, the amount of young people of our own age who, by their friendly acknowledgement to one another, could not be newcomers to this place.

We sat down at the end of the row, about half-way down the

room, Bill being against the wall. I looked above his head and saw a portrait of a man whom I did not recognize. He looked a little French to me, vaguely remembering my history lessons on the French Revolution and seeing pictures of the many aristocrats of that period. There were a lot of other pictures within the church, but from my position I was unable to see them very clearly—another time, I thought, knowing full well that Bill was right, this was indeed the place where we would stay.

I felt very much at ease, the friendly chatter around us gave me a feeling of being part of it all, which I honestly did not feel at the Stonebridge Road church. I took Bill's hand in mine, giving it a little squeeze, and as he looked at me I smiled, and without speaking to one another we both looked towards the altar where the lady who had greeted us so kindly was opening an ornamental wrought-iron gate, which was part of the rostrum, and where she was directing a gentleman to her right. They both sat down and looking around me I became aware of the sudden hush within the building. All that was audible was some very pretty music playing quietly in the background, which magically stopped as the lady stood up. As before we were introduced to the medium and led into the singing of the first hymn.

I can say without any doubt in my mind that the church held us both for as the weeks went by we found our visits becoming more and more frequent. Our children caused us no problems as they had become extremely friendly with a lady who lived almost opposite, who had no children of her own, and practically begged me to allow her the privilege of looking after them whenever I wished. This was indeed an answer to a prayer so we continued as regular churchgoers, Wednesday nights and also Sundays, receiving during this time many messages on our future towards development of our so called gifts.

The lady from the church who had first greeted us was a medium herself—an extremely good one, and it was to our amazement that after some weeks, as we were about to leave the church one evening, she approached us both. "I wonder if you would like to join my development circle which I shall be starting very soon," she said. My hand was still in hers, for she was as her custom, saying goodbyes to each and every one as they passed her at the back of the church. She sensed my surprise and smiled at me. "Do think about it—I've been watching you both and have noted your regular attendance. You will both be more than welcome to come along." "Thank you," I heard Bill say, as I still stood open-mouthed, not believing the words I had just heard. "We would very much like to join," said Bill. I released my hand, embarrassed at having held it so long, and agreed by nodding my head, but I needn't have bothered for I heard the arrangements being directed at Bill. "The first week in September—we shall start at 8 p.m. here in the church."

I stumbled outside, as usual forgetting the little step which was about three inches high. I always seemed to make this trip as if it was put there especially for me, enticing me to fall, for I never saw anyone else make the stupid error. A year later, however, an extension was built on to the house and the tiny step, which had caused me to trip so many times, disappeared.

Driving home from the church that Sunday evening, both of us were very excited. "Development circle, oh Bill, aren't we lucky to be asked," I said. He didn't answer, but he didn't have to. I knew he was pleased as we had been talking about this for some time wondering how we could be invited into a circle, for our knowledge had begun to grow somewhat. We were still very green and our only advancement was what we had learned from the many varied, and sometimes way above us, addresses from the platform. Many of the speakers gave us much food for thought which often, on reaching home, we would analyze, sometimes very critically, for hours on end. We certainly were not going to be taken in or be too gullible, and so as we had grown a little more to understand the world of Spirit we felt the need to investigate further.

"The first week in September," I said, "Why, that's only a couple of weeks off—Friday evenings, that's not a bad night." Bill responded by agreeing with me. "Oh well kid, we've done it now," which sent a thrill right through my body. Once again the car drew up outside our shabby looking residence.

All too soon the great day arrived. I awoke to the noise of a deafening clap of thunder and watched the lightning zig-zag across the small window of the bedroom. Crash went the thunder again. I wasn't surprised. We were due for this, I thought, as I dressed quickly and ran down to the kitchen not surprised to see the children already up and playing with a balloon which was a relic from a birthday party the day before, to which they had been. Neither of them paid the slightest attention to the awful storm which was now at its height. We had, until then, been having some really hot days and the last two nights had been stifling hot. I can remember thinking to myself, Well, I shan't forget this day in a hurry. The storm was indeed a bad one and much damage was reported on the wireless.

Eventually the storm stopped, but the day remained very dark as the clouds rumbled noisily above as if they had had some disagreement. I was hoping that by the evening the roads would have cleared for the disappointment would have been dreadful for us both if we couldn't attend the circle, but of course I had no reason to fear. The evening came and once again we found ourselves approaching the now familiar church. A mixture of excitement and fear held us both in silence, neither of us wanting to exchange our inner feelings. I only knew that from this night my life would change. When, or how, I could not say. I felt strangely comforted at the thought. Whichever way things went I was aware that I would not feel unsure or afraid of the future. I felt as if a long lost guardian angel had come to teach us both new ideas, so much wiser than us, and it felt good, so very good.

We entered the church, the stillness of the place was unfamiliar to me, having by now got used to the many people who attended every meeting, but this night all was quiet. I can remember going on tip-toe along the paving stones so as not to make any noise. The french doors were shut, but I nervously turned the handle, and we went inside. The church was dimly lit and it took a few moments to accustom our eyes to the darkness. I looked around, hearing murmured voices coming from the far end near the rostrum, and made out a circle of chairs. The occupants of the seats looked up, a little startled, I thought.

We were greeted with warmth by a very handsome-looking young man in his early twenties, who took it upon himself to make us welcome, showing us to the vacant chairs within the circle, noticing as I sat down, that most of the sitters were the young people whom we had often seen at the church meetings. The young man caught my eye, as I saw under each chair a glass, containing water. "To revive you," he said, "In case you find the need," then laughed as he saw the obvious terror in my eyes. "Only joking!"

I wondered why there was one chair left vacant, until, before my own thoughts could answer, the medium from the church came in. All went very quiet, not a whisper could be heard. She took her seat and promptly closed her eyes. All those within that little circle did the same—that is, except me. The dim light near the rostrum went even dimmer, almost out, all that was visible were dark shapes. I would have died of fright if at that moment someone had touched me. I certainly would not have been around to tell this story. I could feel my heartbeats and I'm sure all could hear them.

Then a clear voice broke my jangled nerves. A young voice, very soft, but soothing, spoke in an opening prayer, asking for protection for us all and welcoming those from Spirit to join us. I begun to feel a little better, but not daring to open my eyes, they having been shut firmly since the light had been turned down, and so they remained for the complete hour, this being the length of time that we sat. I missed a lot that night due to my stupid weakness of being afraid.

However, I took the opportunity, after the circle had closed, to make friends, for a welcome cup of tea or coffee was available to us. Later I learned that we each took turns in making it. The young man introduced himself and then the other sitters, one being a very pretty young girl, came over to me, anxious to make acquaintance. On hearing her voice, I realised that this was the young lady I had heard earlier. She had beautiful red hair, long and curly. Her eyes were a striking colour of blue which seemed to dance as she spoke. Even though I was myself a female, I just had to admit that she was indeed a stunner, and what was more, she had the personality to go with it. I liked her instantly and within a short time we became very good friends. I was not surprised to find out that she was engaged to the equally attractive young man.

As the weeks went by our relationship with the other members became very close and often after circle we would meet up at the local public house—our main topic of conversation being spirit and its meaning. Whenever we had the chance, whether it be circle night or church night, it became our meeting place and over a pint for the men and a shandy for us girls, we discussed spiritualism hour after hour, never tiring of the subject. As the weeks went by into months, our friendship became very close.

We had now been joined by our very dear friend, Keith, who, at that time, was introduced to us as a man who had many problems and was needing upliftment and help which, of course, he readily received as each member of the circle became more understanding to one another and therefore was able to give much to those in need. Myself I became very much changed. To begin with my appearance was now very important to me. I wanted to look nice and tried hard, making much improvement. I liked the result and found it flattering when a remark was made, especially if it came from our friends within the circle. My home also took on a new look, not immediately but gradually—there seemed, somehow, to be a purpose.

We had settled nicely into the circle, learning many things. We were taught platform behaviour by the medium, taking turns in being the chairman at the services. I enjoyed this very much, as I am sure we all did. It gave me a thrill to see my husband standing there upon the rostrum leading us into prayer. He was also becoming a very good speaker. I noticed this on circle nights when being asked to speak on a given subject, how easily the words seemed to come to him. I, on the other hand, did not seem to be making much progress, although not for the lack of keenness. I enjoyed immensely every moment we were all together, eager to learn.

Our own marriage seemed to take on some sort of change also, we were certainly very much closer, always looking forward to our week-ends so that we could have more time together, sharing our views, discussing different aspects of the spiritualist movement. We were also aware of a possible move around us. The council had notified its tenants, months before, of a new estate to be built in the Cheshunt area. We had hopefully put our name down, although didn't really feel we had much chance and therefore were not enthusiastic of our chances in being selected.

By this time we had been in the circle a good couple of years and my standard of house management had taken on certain changes, giving therefore, to a stranger, a certain warmth to the flat, which as I explained before, was not only untidy but cold. Now visitors came and I enjoyed entertaining. It was during this time I had a visit from the housing officer. The lady informed me, as I answered the door, that she was from the welfare department. "About your application," she said, "May I take a look around."

She critically viewed each room, ending up in my awful kitchen, which now looked remarkably different from the two previous years. I offered her some tea, knowing full well she would refuse. These council people always seemed a little cool and frigid to me, and therefore I was completely taken by surprise when I heard her say that she would love some. We talked together for some time, and I couldn't help noticing she appeared to be having a lot of pain in her leg and surprised myself when I asked if she had ever considered having healing for it. She had not, but was not offended by my asking her. I could tell, however, that she had no intention of finding out, but certainly by her tone of voice was impressed that I should even care about her. We talked a little more and then she was gone, giving me no hint as to whether we would indeed be listed for one of the new houses.

A few months after the visit of the welfare officer, it was with great delight that we received an official letter informing us that we had been selected for a new three-bedroom house in Cheshunt. I remember cuddling the children, letting them enjoy the happiness and thrill that I was feeling, laughing with them as I told them that we would be having a real bathroom of our very own, with hot water, lots of rooms, but most of all, a garden—not an old backyard like the one they knew. Their whoops of delight as they saw how happy their mum was and how she kept answering their many questions as to where were we going, how big was the bathroom, would we have our own street door, was Cheshunt a long way away, had to be seen to be believed. "Yes, yes," I kept saying, laughing with them. Bill was delighted—just as much as I had been, and joined in with the general noise and excitement of it all.

It took us nearly a year before we actually moved and at times we began to think may be it would never happen, although the many Spirit messages we had received always indicated that this move would take place. We never really thought, or expected, that it would take so long. Throughout this time of waiting we continued going to church and circle each week. Our friendship with the circle became so close that we were each like brother and sister to one another. We all became advanced in our knowledge and were now able to answer any questions of newcomers who came to the church. My husband, and our good friend, Keith, helped to build the extension, of which I spoke earlier, at the church, not realizing at that time that they were indeed leaving some sort of monument, as they cemented the bricks and built the window frames.

So much was around us at that time as we moved and quickly settled in our new house. All our friends from the church came, even the medium, which to us was indeed an honour. She gave us a cutting of honeysuckle from the garden of the church to plant in our own cherished garden, and that honeysuckle, to this day, blooms every year, reminding me of her with kind thoughts, for although I did not know then, we were soon to break away from the church. I think my world would have caved in as I loved her and the church so much. It was part of us and therefore I thought nothing would be able to break that link.

Whilst the move we had made and also the extension to the church was going on we still continued our development. I still appeared not to be getting anywhere, unable to say much when asked during circle, but would envy the others when they spoke as they were inspired by their Spirit guides. Although I tried very hard nothing seemed to happen for me, that is until one particular night. The medium had been, over the past few weeks, encouraging us, in pairs, to go on to the rostrum during circle, one to speak and the other in turn, to give off inspired clairvoyance, the speaker taking his or her seat to the right of the rostrum.

"I want, tonight, Sheila and Bill to take the platform," she said. I cringed. It was bad enough sitting in the circle not being able to speak let alone going up there, I thought, looking up at the altar. However, I found myself walking up to the rostrum, opening the pretty gates, which always gave me the impression of the Gates of Heaven. I certainly needed some great power with me tonight, I thought, as I found myself sitting where the speaker would sit. Bill came over to me and whispered, "You've gone to the wrong side." I refused to move and stubbornly I said I was staying put, not understanding why. I just couldn't control my attitude. The medium was aware something was amiss and in a strict voice asked what the problem was. I heard Bill say that I had taken the wrong chair. Without turning, for her back was towards us, she said, "Where you are you must stay." So Bill resigned himself to this fact and took the other side of the platform.

From then on something most strange happened to me. I'll

explain it to the best of my knowledge, for this experience has now become second nature to me, but sitting there that night was like being at the dentist's and being administered gas, hearing voices at first softly, but then becoming louder, with the room beginning to revolve around me, and then spinning until sudden oblivion.

I came back to reality, badly shaken, unaware of the surroundings. I knew I was terribly dry. I drank a complete tumbler of water, almost in one gulp. The medium quickly closed the circle and then I began to relax. I was told of a spirit who had used me whilst being in a tranced condition. I was bewildered, as before that moment nothing had happened to me during all the time I had sat in circle, and yet, without warning, I had been taken into a trance. I don't think I was over-keen on it at first. It all frightened me a little.

I gratefully drank my coffee, not wishing, as was usual, to join in the general conversation with our friends. The medium came over to me. "Come with me," she said, taking me into the little room which was used for the mediums serving the church, "I want you to listen to what I have to say. You have a rare gift and you can take or reject it at your free-will, but if you chose to develop this gift, I advise you to sit with only those who will give you love, who will be unselfish and encourage this truly precious gift that is yours, should you wish to use it, true trance is rare. That's why you have sat so long, as you thought getting nowhere. They were preparing you and now, with love, you have something wonderful. Don't be foolish with it, develop carefully, keeping only those around you who care and are close to you."

I thanked her for the advice and joined our friends, feeling as we left that night, a great excitement. We were going to meet the following evening at my home as a get-together, which had now become very regular. We would play records, discuss Spirit and, yes, often make fun, laughing at ourselves, pretending we were some famous medium, by doing an impersonation.

Even by this time of our development we still saw many flaws and were very critical, so when they all arrived that Saturday evening, it was not surprising, having told them what our medium had said about my gift and I should only sit with those who loved me, that it seemed perfectly natural that we should conduct a circle there and then, being with friends who were only too willing to give their love to me, we arranged a circle, conducting it correctly, starting in prayer. Together we sat in serenity, and as had happened the night before, the same thing took place. I remember nothing, only the terrible dryness on coming back.

"Was it good?" I said, "Did the same guide speak?" I was now eager to know. "It was super," said Keith. "Absolutely," they each agreed. "We've been talking to many spirits through you, it's incredible," I heard my friends saying, with eagerness. We all agreed we would not, for the moment, let the medium know what we had been up to. Strange, but we each felt a little guilty about having the circle. Although it was all perfectly innocent, once again our thirst for knowledge would be the only reason for that evening's happenings.

We arrived at the church the following Friday and were greeted by Keith, who was looking very unhappy. "I've told her," he said, "I couldn't help myself. I was up here in the week, helping with the extension, and blurted it out. I'm so sorry, but I thought she would be pleased, but she was so cross." "Oh dear," I said, "We are in trouble now."

We walked slowly into the church, where instead of the happy chatter which was the usual scene, all was quiet. Not one of us spoke, only nodding to one another as we waited for the medium to join us, a bit like naughty children waiting for punishment. As soon as our teacher joined us she looked around at her pupils with a quick quizzical look, probably unnerved herself by the deadly silence which greeted her. After the opening prayer was said we were asked, as always, to be linked with our Spirit friends, but due to the fact that her feeling of being so cross with us, as Keith had already warned, created an uncomfortable atmosphere, we all fidgeted on our chairs.

She, of course, sensed this atmosphere and said, "All right, who will speak first, what is wrong?" Bill spoke, saying, "You know what is wrong," and continued to say, "I can't understand why you are so cross with us. True it's early days and perhaps we should have taken more care with Sheila, but it was with your advice that we were led to believe that it was essential to sit with people that would give her love—this circle are our friends, whom we love dearly, as I know they love us, surely this was not wrong to sit together. We followed your strict rules. Why should you be so cross." Bill's voice sounded very hurt. I wanted to cry.

I then heard the words, "Sheila did not understand. I did not expect her to use this circle outside of my control. I'm sorry if I have given her the wrong impression." Before Bill answered I put my hand in his, and spoke, surprised how clear-cut my voice was. "I have caused this circle distress, even though I feel at this time misled, it is with great regret that I must resign for I shall always feel that in some way I have spoilt what we have together and this circle will never be the same to me again. What we did I felt was right—therefore, as from this night, I shall resign, but very regretfully."

I stopped, for I knew I was going to cry. I couldn't believe that this was really happening to me. I loved the circle so much and over the years had grown to love and trust the medium. Why was it wrong, why did she tell me to sit only with those who loved me. Had I not done just that. I knew no other people willing to give of themselves to help me. All these thoughts were leaping about my troubled mind that night. I felt deeply and spiritually hurt. After a while the circle closed and Bill and I left. To me it was the end and I felt as if I had been thrown out of a nest, like a young bird leaving before its time.

"Oh God, help me," I said, over and over again, on the journey home. After the initial shock, I insisted that Bill should continue going to the circle. At least that way his development would not be held up because of me. Although he was very reluctant to go, he did so. I in turn, tried to make contact with Spirit and asked their help by giving me some kind of lead, but nothing seemed to be forthcoming.

During this time I had also left my daily occupation, mainly due to the travelling back and fro to Tottenham. I decided to get something local and was successful in obtaining a very nice little job almost on my doorstep. It was at the top end of the estate in a wages office. From the beginning I enjoyed the work immensely and being so near home I was able to check at lunch-time that the little puppy dog which we had acquired was safe and sound. It was a beautiful corgi, whom we all adored. I am sure that little dog saved me from going completely out of my mind as I was able to express my feelings to her. She would sit on my lap and appear to understand me, giving me so much comfort. I discussed with her many ideas, and Lady, this being the name we had given her, would snuggle her long nose against my neck and shuffle her tiny body as if in answer to me. I would eat a hurried sandwich, check that all was well with her, and then hasten back to the office, allowing myself approximately five minutes in which to return before the end of the lunch break.

However, on one particular day I must have misjudged the time and arrived back to the office a good twenty minutes before time. The two girls I worked with looked up most surprised as I walked into the tiny office. I pulled up the flap, which allowed me to enter, and I made for my desk. As this was a wages office we had a counter which kept out other staff. "You're back early," they both said, simultaneously. "We were just discussing the stars," said my colleagues. "Do you think there is anything in it?" they asked, "Only we've always been interested and its uncanny how things really do seem to happen, probably its just coincidence."

Without realising it, I heard myself say, "It's not a coincidence I can assure you, I am a medium." The words were out and I couldn't retract the statement. The two girls looked at me incredulously. I knew I would have to back up my statement and felt, for one moment, panic. I mentally reached out to my Spirit friends, whom I had learnt of through circle, to help me. Apart from my gift of trance my ability to contact Spirit was, until that precise moment, non-existent.

At that very moment the office manager came in. I remember feeling, thank God, I've been saved, but to my horror, heard the eager voice of one of my colleagues saying, "Tell him Sheila, what you just told us." "I'm a medium," I said, amazed at the cocky attitude of my voice. "Well now, that's very interesting," said my boss, "Tell me something about myself."

Here we go, I thought, but was surprised when I started to speak. I found I knew quite a lot about him and was able to describe certain relatives of his who had passed away some years before. To say he was impressed would be an understatement. He was shocked into silence which gave my work friends the opportunity of asking about themselves. This I was also able to do without any hesitation. After that lunch break I found that the word had spread throughout the whole building and I was the centre of attention. Having spent the majority of my spare time with one or another of the many staff employed at this building, I found that I was amazed and delighted at the accuracy of my clairvoyance. I could not, of course, let them know this as they said, "Oh Sheila, you are so clever." I would smile to myself, thinking, you don't know how much, and mentally give a silent prayer of thanks.

The days went quickly by, each one giving me more experience of my clairvoyant gift, but I was still very uncertain regarding what I was to do and often at night became very moody. Bill found me this way one night on coming home from circle, which he was still attending. "There's going to be a bazaar next week, and there's a couple of vacancies left for private sittings, why don't you let me book one for you, it could help, you know!" Bill was so kind, always worried about me. Before I had time to answer him, he continued, knowing what I was about to say "There are going to be two visiting mediums so what has happened to you won't be known to them." "All right," I said, "Maybe I'll get some help, I've certainly asked and prayed for an answer."

On the following Saturday I found myself, once again, on the familiar grounds of the church. I avoided, as much as I could, getting close to the medium, like a naughty child afraid of being chastised. Whilst I was waiting I sat on a spare chair that had been placed as a door-stop, keeping an eye open for the rush of people that were expected. I watched many of them buying refreshments and took in all the hustle and bustle around. I was also kept amused by watching the antics of a little boy who was determined to have his own way, picking up with his grubby little hand, two chocolate biscuits, and grinning, very self-satisfied, when his mother, with a sigh, paid up. Children, I thought, they really do cause in their own little way, many headaches to their parents. The little boy reminded me very much of my own son, who was probably at this very moment playing my mother up in much the same way.

"You're next, he is waiting for you in there," Bill said, bringing me back to earth with a start, directing me to the little mediums room at the end of the church. I hurriedly made my way to my client, having difficulty getting past the white elephant stall which had attracted many people and was causing quite a commotion of traffic. I eventually reached the door, and knocking, went quickly in. A rather elderly gentleman greeted me with a warm handshake. I sat down on the vacant chair and waited.

Please, please, I said mentally, let this man help me. "You are very unhappy," he said, "Spiritually confused, you feel let down. Let me tell you child, you are not to blame. The time has come for you to spread your wings. Do not blame your teacher, she is unaware and has no control. Spirit wanted the break, it was time, and this was the only way to move you into the direction they wished you to go. You must show to others your spirit talents and, like a bird, a fledgling, make your beginning. I shall give you at the end of this sitting an address where you will make contact and explain your need to work and where you will tell them of your willingness to take a little test. Experienced mediums will be able to give you an honest opinion of your abilities to work on a platform."

I could have quite easily kissed this man for his help and guidance which he had so generously given to me. "Thank you," I said, "I will indeed follow the advice that has been given." I shook his hand gratefully. "You will do well, my dear," he said, as I left the room clutching the precious piece of paper on which was written the address of the new opening being offered to me, and where hopefully, I would find an answer.

Bill was waiting for me as I came out. "Any help?" he said enquiringly. "Oh yes," I smiled at him, "Very much so." "I shouldn't be very long, my stall has practically sold out, why not give me a hand," he said. "No dear, I'll wait in the car, don't worry, I'll be O.K., you carry on." The noise in the building making me shout a little to be heard. I heard Keith's familiar voice, saying, "Roll up, roll up, ladies and gentlemen, buy your lucky ticket here." I took Bill's keys, laughing with him as we saw Keith's extremely funny look. He was wearing a very old black top hat. I gave him a friendly wave and left the church, noticing as I did so, that the bunting had fallen down from its position above the gateway, it was now draped half in and half out of a puddle. I picked it up and hung it on a large nail which was sticking out of the fence. I remember thinking about the last bazaar I had attended where I had put the flags and bunting away and tidied up the old boxes which contained them, ready to be put away until next time. I swallowed as I felt a lump in my throat.

I hurriedly got into our car and whilst I was waiting for Bill I looked at the address on the paper which had been given to me.

Bina Gardens, London. I wanted there and then to write, eager to get started. Me, to work on a church platform. Would I be good enough, I wondered. These thoughts remained with me during the coming weeks of waiting for a reply to my letter, for it would seem that my spiritual path had come to a sudden halt. Bill, by this time, had also left the circle due to the illness of the medium. It appeared that we were both at a complete full stop where Spirit was concerned. Keith was also missing the circle very much and used to spend that same evening with us and so it was natural that we should sit in the form of a circle, just the three of us, mostly giving absent healing to those we knew to be sick.

It was during one of these sittings that my very dear loving guide, Lucille, made her presence known to us, and has, to this day, given upliftment, guidance and love to those who have listened to her simple words of wisdom.

During this time of search by Bill and myself, a letter arrived inviting me to attend a fledgling meeting where there would be others who were also eager to begin platform work. We would be, apparently, given a little time to demonstrate before an invited audience. I went along, feeling very nervous, but need not have done so, for everyone was very kind. We were asked to simply be ourselves, to speak up clearly and display our talents, and at a later date we would receive constructive criticism of help from certain members of the congregation who would be assessing our platform presentation in respect of our psychic abilities, if, in their opinion we were ready to work on a church platform as new workers.

While we waited for an answer from that evening's demonstration, we continued our little circle, and were beginning to have some wonderful results. Many spirits visited us and gave proof of their identity, deliberately giving names and dates for us to check. The most exciting Spirit that contacted us was a young doctor who informed us his name was John Luke Irwin Lenon of Edinburgh, Scotland. We investigated his existence through the British Medical Association, who, after some time, did indeed confirm that a doctor of that name was registered in the year 1884. So we were now becoming very much more spiritually developed through this tiny circle.

I heard, in due course, favourably of my demonstration and was advised by three different critics to pursue and gain experience within the churches. Having this now in my possession I wrote to a number of local spiritualist churches asking to be given the opportunity to work and to give service. Only one replied, which was a small church in Edmonton. They gave me my first chance, which was successful, and from this I had many approach me from other churches. It was then that I persuaded Bill to take the addresses for me. Speaking, even to this day, is not for me. I feel that it is most important that the speaker should be good at the job and many newcomers fail to understand spirit simply because they have not been able to receive clear, inspired understanding and have left confused, sometimes completely with the wrong impression of the Spirit world.

So together we began to work, going to churches, the months rolling by, our experience showing from the platform as we became more attuned to our Spirit contacts. Our circle at home was also very strong, still only the three of us. Every week we sat, growing closer and spiritually developing our gifts. A couple of years went by and we were all satisfied with our progression. Up to this time my family were aware of our interest in spiritualism and knew that we travelled around quite a lot, but were not over-enthusiastic, only I think, noting my definite change of appearance which was to them, in itself, an improvement and was not such an embarrassment.

We were at my mother's one particular Sunday morning, a little concerned because we had a meeting at St. Alban's Church that evening and Bill's car had broken down. My brother was there and he kindly offered to take us. I was so relieved and thanked him for his kindness. Funny, but we were as children very close, but over the years had not made much contact with one another. One would say we were poles apart. So that evening, driving off to church with my brother, made me very content. He asked many questions on the journey and we answered happily, pleased that he showed such interest. Although he had decided to sit outside the church, on our arrival, after my gentle persuasion, he said he would go into the church and sit at the back. It was with a sense of achievement, on my part, to have him sitting there.

The evening went well and as usual I proceeded, at random, to speak to members of the congregation, when a compelling force made me stop. I apologised to the audience, ''I must speak to my brother, who is sitting at the back." Had he at that time possessed a gun he would have shot me, but I stood my ground and said, "You will be up on this platform working with us within a very short time." He stared at me and said in a very loud voice, "I think not." I broke from him and the service continued.

After the singing of the last hymn I noticed my brother hurriedly leaving the church. I was wondering what sort of reception we would receive from him. However, I was pleasantly surprised and relieved, for on the journey back his interest seemed to have increased, and on depositing us at home agreed to join us in circle the next night that we would be sitting. So the very next week my brother joined us, his wife not inclined to become involved. "You go in, I'll keep an eye on the children," she said, having brought their own son with them. "I'll be perfectly all right," she assured me as we went into my little room, which had originally been built as an annexe room for prams, etc., but we found it just right for our circle, being small and compact. We also used it as a healing sanctuary. I've always loved that little room. Somehow you can feel the peace as you enter.

Lucille spoke, welcoming my brother. She also informed him that his wife would be joining him the next time that he sat with us. He said this was doubtful due to her already telling him earlier that she did not want to be mixed up with that sort of thing and was not really happy at my brother's obvious interest. Lucille, however, was adamant. No pressure shall be put upon her, she will ask to join you all, which, of course, was the case. My sister-in-law became the fifth member of our circle the very next week and our search for the truth continued.

This time as a group.

CHAPTER THREE

THE PAM GROUP

Life within my home took on a much different look than it had done a few years earlier. I now took great pains in the general appearance of the house. We found that we never lacked company—which I enjoyed immensely. Bill had changed too—he was no longer the quiet little boy who sat in the corner—due, no doubt, to taking so many services. He had mastered the art of speaking and was able to converse on more-or-less any given subject—which made him quite good company to have around.

Many people came to visit us—not all, let me add, spiritualists, but certainly a great percentage of our guests showed some interest—knowing what we were. It was usual for the evening to turn into deep discussion, with people interested to hear our views. Sometimes we would sit half the night in healthy discussion and it was not unusual to hear the dawn chorus when our friends left the house.

It was in this atmosphere that my brother and his wife first joined us—enjoying the friendly people who were forever in and out. My brother has a wonderful personality—he was always at his best when in company. He became so full of enthusiasm—he had taken Spirit almost without question—and those who didn't know him would have been amazed as to how little knowledge he had on the subject. He was, indeed, well and truly hooked—like a drug one might say—anxious and enthralled by the wonder of it all—and within a very short time settled to the development circle, eager to learn. Indeed, he was a studious pupil.

His wife, however, took things much more the reverse—showing caution—and she, being an introvert, found expression of her own feelings hard to explain. She was not prepared to take things at face value and often became hurt, due to not being understood, and sometimes by saying the wrong thing—often causing cross words between herself and her husband. This was a pity, but it was obvious she felt much stronger and, unlike her husband, she needed time to digest this new experience. She was not prepared to accept Spirit so readily. However, my sister-in-law was prepared to learn and became herself an interested sitter. We all seemed to blend together really well and found, as from our previous experience when in the church circle, that we had become very, very close.

We would all go to a meeting together when Bill and I were taking a service—and they, being able to sit close by, gave me every encouragement—at the same time enjoying the church meeting. This also gave them outsiders' views—apart from ours—where they were able to ask questions of the many spiritualists that they met. It gave them experience—which was essential—for the coming months would not have materialized had we known in advance.

The five of us went practically everywhere together—finding great enjoyment in whatever we were doing. The circle became stronger and stronger—and we had now been joined by a German Spirit doctor who, with Lucille, became teachers to us. We would discuss after each circle the many different lessons put before us to find out how each had progressed. I, at this time was unable to give any views, as at each sitting I was taken into a trance condition—so I would usually make the tea—taking my time—as it always seemed to take me a while to become accustomed to the material things around me. I would join them a little later—with great interest—to learn of the contents of the circle.

It was during one of those evenings—as I came through with the tray of coffee—that I became aware of overloud eager voices. I placed the tray down on the coffee table—having difficulty moving a large glass ashtray which was in the way—noticing that nobody was about to come to my aid. They were much too enthralled in what had taken place. I sometimes used to feel very hurt—for it was as if I wasn't there—this often being the case due to my being in a tranced condition. Therefore, unintentionally, I was not included as part of the development circle—and I often felt an outsider.

What's all the excitement, I enquired—as I stopped their conversation in mid-air. They each looked up at me, a little surprised by my interruption. "You'll never guess what the doctor has in mind," said my brother—wide-eyed at the information he held within—and by his voice I could tell that he was a little scared. He licked his lips nervously—looking around at each one of us—and then blurted out, "He wants us to hire a hall—the doctor wants us to hire a hall." He had answered my question before I had uttered a word. "The doctor," I said, "What for?" "Not sure, exactly," said Bill. "But we are too look around and find ourselves a decent sized hall and then book it," said Keith, interrupting Bill.

"That sounds a bit adventurous," I said—realising that none of us had any experience outside of the churches—and at that particular time only Bill and I were developed enough—having done public demonstrations on a very small scale. "When are we to do this?" I asked them. "Well, as soon as possible, at least look around for a suitable hall," said my brother, "Only then will the doctor explain what Spirit wishes us to do and he will direct us accordingly." "Sounds quite intriguing," said Keith, "Don't you think?" looking at me with those eyes which always made me laugh. Such a lovely nature—one always felt so warm in his presence. I smiled at him, "I'm not so sure, I'll feel better when I know what we are to do with this so-called hall," I said practically.

Having by this time, over a number of years, gained respect as a worker and was, to be honest, a little afraid of Bill's and my reputation—I was not prepared to let us make fools of ourselves. I knew the thought would not surface, but it was there, and at that time I meant it. My sister-in-law remained strangely quiet—giving no hint as to her own feelings—so it was to my surprise when she remarked on what we should wear. She showed no fear or apprehension about the proposed service which was obviously what Spirit had in mind. "We ought to wear something dark—both of us —navy blue perhaps?" I was astonished. I had always admired the way my sister-in-law looked—she always paying great attention to the appearance of her dress. At that moment it seemed hardly the time to discuss our apparel. I smiled at her, "Let's worry about that when and if we're able to get that far." Not having any idea at that time how one went about looking for halls—also how much it would cost.

Money was an important factor in those days—and it was difficult enough to live—to find money for other things was, indeed, a very severe problem. However, we agreed that I should investigate the possibility, and if the price was reasonable we would share the expense, equally five ways. That very next morning I began my search—enquiring at our local library—who suggested the possibility of the grammar school—which was close by our estate and yet very central—being in the position of close proximity to the railway station and bus stop—it also housed a large car park. Armed with the school's telephone number, and feeling pretty pleased with myself having got so far so soon. I went into work very late that morning—deciding that I would ring at lunch time and make, if necessary, an appointment. My colleagues greeted me with enthusiasm as I arrived—having already telephoned to inform them that I would be late. I hurriedly explained what I had been up to and then dismissed the subject quickly.

In those days computers were only talked about—wages, therefore, were still worked upon manually and a deadline was necessary. Staff received their wages weekly and one had little time to waste. Everybody was important—and wasting time chatting would create all sorts of problems. I settled down—took the wages sheets and tax code and began working steadily, trying hard, very hard, to concentrate—having so much on my mind. I wonder how much it will cost, I thought. I suppose I'd better say it's for a religious meeting. I shook myself as the figures danced up at me—compelling me to pay attention. The figure four I had written down three times—and they looked as if each number had an arrow drawn ready to fire. I rubbed them out quickly and begun again—this time concentrating with effort.

When the lunch-time bell at last pealed out its friendly tune, I flew from the office, nearly breaking my arm in the process—having not secured the counter-flap. As I hurriedly left it came down with a bang—dangerously missing my arm by inches. "Sorry," I shouted back. I saw looks of dismay at the deafening noise—and I was gone.

I seemed to be home within minutes—and I was breathing heavily as I turned the key. I was, as usual, greeted with great excitement by my corgi—who by this time had grown into a beautiful little dog. Having had her some years—we now had a wonderful relationship—she never failed to delight me—seeming to know whatever mood I was in and adapting accordingly. This day, on entering the front door, she immediately sensed my eagerness and, after greeting her, I went quickly to the back door so that I could be left without any hindrance from her to do what I had to do. "You are a darling," I said, as I quickly bent down to kiss her—opening the back door. With an excited bark she bounded into the garden.

I put the kettle on and took the already prepared sandwich out of the refrigerator—not bothering with a plate—unwrapped it from the greaseproof paper—and ate ravenously. Now for the call. I read out loud the number and repeated it as I dialled each digit on the receiver. It rang for sometime—in fact, I was just about to put the receiver down, when I heard a voice repeating the number I had just dialled. "Could I speak to the secretary?" I said, in my best telephone voice. "Speaking," came back the answer, "Can I help you?" "Oh yes, I do hope so," I said, in my friendliest manner—and then proceeded to ask her the possibility of hiring the school hall for a religious meeting. What type of religious meeting, came back the reply. I hesitated—now comes the crunch—I thought. "A spiritualists' meeting," I said to her. "I would have to have a word with the headmaster—may I ring you back?" "Why certainly," I said, but at the same time thinking, she won't. "Could you ring back about this time tomorrow," I asked. "Of course," she replied, and promptly with an "until then," the phone went dead.

I stood there some time—pondering and trying to get some clue from her voice. No, she definitely did not seem surprised at the nature of my proposed use of the hall. Oh, well, let's see, I thought, at least I've done my part.

The very next day, as arranged, the secretary did ring and, yes, the head had no objections to us having the use of his school—providing we would use a Saturday for the meeting—this being the only day convenient to him. I agreed to this arrangement—having also been told the very reasonable rate—and agreed that I would pop along to the school as soon as we had a suitable date in mind. Up until then I had no idea when, indeed for what, we were going to use the place for exactly.

The following circle night, we were told the intention was to demonstrate an evening of clairvoyance and healing together—this being foreign to us as very few mediums at that time used both these psychic gifts together. Speaking and clairvoyance, yes, but never healing and clairvoyance. Our Spirit doctor, however, was adamant that this was what would be required of us—many questions having been asked of him—because at that time only two of the five had ever worked on a platform—and there was a great deal of hesitation, when I listened to the tape recording of the doctor, each one expressing their views.

"The power will be given if you do as we ask of you," I heard the doctor say, "I have faith in your ability—do you have faith in us?" I then heard Lucille's voice—clear and comforting, "Do not be afraid, all will be well—do as the doctor asks of you. Through the meeting many will hear of your work—arrange this meeting now—and help will be given to you," the tape ended.

"O.K.," I said, "What now?" "Well, it looks like we need to organize ourselves," Bill said. We each agreed, nodding our heads. "I think I know someone who will get the tickets made up," said my brother. A date is the most important—I was looking through the diary—better give ourselves time. The weeks sped by—a friend of ours offered to tape some organ music—which we accepted readily. I had confirmed the date at the school, but did not see the size of the hall. I only knew we were to use the assembly hall and that rows of chairs would be arranged for us by the caretaker.

Everything went well—we decided on some sort of a programme—keeping very much to the familiar church services—except, of course, that healing would also be demonstrated. The idea was that I would give the clairvoyance—Bill would give some sort of talk about the evening—and Keith would close with prayer. So in turn we would all play a part in the service—which was being asked of us by Spirit.

The tickets were printed—I rang different churches which we had already served—telling them of the proposed evening—informing them that tickets were on sale. All too soon the evening arrived—with us having, to our dismay, sold only two tickets. "Not to worry," I said, trying to sound unconcerned, "There will probably be a lot of people buy them at the door—we've told such a lot." Each of us looked very smart—we girls wearing navy blue dresses and white cardigans—The men in their Sunday suits.

Although the school was only just around the corner, we piled into my brother's car—with Bill following, carrying all the tape equipment, programmes, etc. We arrived a good hour before the appointed time so that we could organize ourselves—laughing at the telephone call I had received earlier from an electrician who, in all innocence, had asked if we required any special effects. It was in this mood—laughing at the thought of weird lighting—that we arrived at the school. Piling out of the car—and laughing nervously—as we realised we were there.

The caretaker, who was waiting for us, began explaining the position he had arranged the chairs—taking care that we noted the hard work he had put in. We followed him along the smart corridor. "Expecting a full house?" his Irish voice sounded hollow in the long passageway. "Probably," my brother said, trying to sound very important. We came to a pair of swing doors. "Well, here we are," said the caretaker. He pushed them open. Complete disbelief hit us like a thunderclap. I saw, from the corner of my eye, my sister-in-law make the sign of the cross. Keith went white with horror—my brother was, for once, tongue-tied. Bill, as yet, still had to see the scene which was before us. A hall—which held a thousand chairs—each neatly put into close rows—and having a centre aisle. The stage itself was as huge as some churches we had been into and we, up to that moment, had sold only two tickets!

"I'll leave you—should you want anything you'll find me outside," the little man was looking at us oddly—for none of us had said a word since entering the hall. My thoughts were interrupted—hearing, "Good God;" coming from Bill's throat—he was half in and half out of the doorway, heavily burdened with programmes and hymn sheets. "Did you know it was this size?" he said to me accusingly, "It's gigantic." The caretaker, having heard, quickly made his exit. "I never realized," I said, "The secretary only said the assembly hall—that seemed O.K. to me—I wasn't to know it would be this size—I've never been in here before. Oh dear, what a mess, what shall we do?" "We must carry on, that's what we must do," said Bill. "Spirit said many people would hear about this—they certainly will," he said sarcastically, "A fiasco!"

I knew he didn't mean it, his nerves were getting the better of him, but what had I done. If only I could have hidden away somewhere, I felt so responsible having hired the damned hall. "It's a lovely stage—come up here and take a look." My brother was walking about investigating the walls, mostly looking for electric points to put the tape recorder on. "Ah, here we are, he said," triumphantly. We each followed one another on to the stage. From this angle the rows and rows of chairs looked much more foreboding than the view from the door. "Good evening, ladies and gentlemen," said my brother in a loud voice, "I don't think we shall need the microphone—pretty good sound effect from up here, go to the back of the hall, Keith, and tell me if you can hear all right." "Right," said Keith, jumping down from the stage and obediently going to the back of the hall. "No problem—I hear you perfectly," he said, then laughed hysterically. "Oh, lor, what a carry on!" With that comment he quickly retreated. I knew he was making for the gents—a particular habit appertaining to Keith when his nerves were on edge.

I looked at my sister-in-law's face. I could read from her expression that she was definitely very scared, and I am sure I heard her saying quietly to herself the Lord's Prayer. Bill, however, having said his piece, was now busy sorting out the equipment. "Right, ready," he said to my brother, and then I heard the sweet organ music sounds playing. "Fine," said Bill, "All set—well all we can do now is wait," as the tape was set ready for action.

We then retreated out to the playground for a cigarette, walking up and down nervously. I noticed the very smart board on which an arrow pointed towards the hall. "Demonstration of Clairvoyance and Healing"—the words standing out so beautiful and clear. Not a soul was about and it was twenty minutes to go to the appointed hour. Keith, during all this time, was in and out of the gents as if he was suffering from dysentery instead of first night nerves. I saw the headlights of a car and I made my retreat back to the hall. It wouldn't look good to be seen smoking, and I was surprised to find the rest of the group following me. We went on to the stage, behind the curtains, and peeped out—hearing noisy footsteps entering the hall. Afraid that we might be noticed we sat it out behind the curtains, sweating. We could hear murmured voices. "At least someone is out there," I whispered to the others. "Five minutes to zero," Bill said. I said a little prayer. "Please be with us." Then it was time. We walked out together.

We had arranged a table on the centre of the stage, with chairs placed around the back. The tape-recording equipment was on a smaller table to the left. We took our seats, not at that point daring to look out. The music began, giving a kind of peace to our shattered nerves, then my brother, who we had appointed as chairman, welcomed the congregation. I could hear his well-rehearsed words. "How pleasing to see so many of you here this night," he went on. I looked at the two rows that we had managed to fill, and I quickly did a count—thirty-nine. Odd number, I remember thinking, and they filled just two lines of chairs. Just to give a little idea of the expanse of the hall.

Well, we had started—the show must go on, I thought, swallowing my disappointment, and so we continued through our service, keeping to our programme until, that is, I started the clairvoyance. I was, as usual, giving messages when I was surprised to hear Bill's voice interrupting my message. I stood back, allowing him to take over, then continued on when he had finished. I was really astonished to hear Keith's voice, he also wanting to give clairvoyance. This to me was quite a shock, but I battled on. We then demonstrated healing, each taking a part of the procedure—laying of hands—putting the patients at their ease—everyone of us playing a part. Yes, that evening, even though so poorly attended, was a success, for as predicted from our Spirit friends, many would hear of us.

At the end of the evening, as we were collecting our things together, a gentleman from the audience approached us. "I'm very impressed by your demonstration," he said, after introducing himself as the president of a church in Enfield. "The sincerity of the service has left me very interested in your new approach to demonstrating the many aspects of spiritualism—I would be honoured if you would conduct the same service in my church one evening." Of course we were absolutely thrilled, and gladly left our telephone number with him. Leaving the school that night, were five very satisfied people. The fact that there was so very few who had turned up did not mean a thing now—we were happy—we had been asked to work inside a spiritualist church for a special evening. This indeed was certainly a bonus. None of us had thought for one minute that church would be interested in us as a group.

When we sat again on circle night, the following week, our Spirit doctor spoke with enthusiasm. "Beautiful," he said, "You worked together as a team—this is our intention. We want you to continue always to work together, the way will be shown to you, opportunities will come, seek and you will find the way.'' Lucille then spoke these following words which, I might add were repeated so many, many times, ''Stay as you are, do not change, be yourselves—this will be your only failure. You have been given something beautiful, to work as a group, but to be as one—a rare gift indeed, Many will admire you and many will be your enemies. You will travel far and wide. Remember, stay as you are!''

I switched the tape off, deep in thought. Lucille's words still lingered in my ears. Change, why should we change, I thought, little realizing, in those early days, that this indeed would happen many years later. We each settled down to our weekly circle and our regular healing night, where our house was open to any who needed help. There were many interesting people during that time, and our enthusiasm to work was very apparent. I left the wages office and started working as an auxiliary nurse at our local hospital. I found the work deeply satisfying and was able, on many occasions, to give spiritual healing, unbeknown to my superiors.

Our group was becoming a little restless—now finding the circle and healing not enough, and very often referred back to the demonstration. I knew, somehow, that is was up to my husband and I to do something if, as spirit expressed, their will was for us to work as a group. Experience was very necessary. True the night at the school had been successful, but we had a long way to go, and the only way was through every opportunity to demonstrate our gifts together. I browsed through our diary, where we kept our church bookings, for by this time Bill and I were fairly well-known due to our serving many churches over the past years. I noticed that we had a date booked for the coming Sunday, and smiled, for the very church happened to be St. Alban's. As was usual the medium's secretary would either write or ring a day or so before the booking to confirm. That's it, I thought, drawing a circle round the letters, I'll wait for them to ring, which was probable because of our reliability, usually on the same day of the meeting. They wouldn't dare refuse me, I pondered. Too late for them to get anyone else, we'll all do the service together. Why, I'm brilliant, I thought, what a super idea.

I explained to the group what I had in mind. I wouldn't have said they were over-enthusiastic—possibly because the meeting was only a few days away, giving them little time to think, but knowing that they had each expressed their views about their keenness in working on a platform, did not dare remark, other than, "Do you think the church will like it?" "I don't see that they will have much option," I replied, "It will be too late for them to replace Bill."

As if, at that moment, listening to our conversation, the telephone rang. I was a little astonished to hear the voice at the other end saying, "This is St. Alban's secretary speaking, just ringing to confirm Sunday's booking with you and your husband." Composing myself quickly, having by sign language informed the rest of the group to whom I was speaking, holding in at the same time my strong desire to laugh, seeing the shocked expressions on their faces, I answered "I'm so pleased that you have rung, I've just this very moment been speaking about your church." The secretary interrupted me at this point, saying in a very anxious voice, "Oh, I do hope you can make it!" "Oh yes," I assured her, "Only we are experimenting with something new in the way of platform work, and I wonder if you would mind if I brought our circle along to demonstrate." I could tell she was a little apprehensive, "Don't worry, it shall be the same order of service, just that there will be five instead of two workers." "Well, in that case I see no reason why not, certainly Mrs. Macey, we shall look forward to it."

I sighed with relief as I replaced the receiver. "How's that then," I said, to the others who were still looking open-mouthed, unbelieving what they had just heard. "That's extraordinary," said my brother, bringing them back to reality. "Look," I said, "I'm not sure how this is going to work, we certainly won't be able to demonstrate healing, it will have to be the usual type service, otherwise we are going to upset an awful lot of people." Bill, who had been sitting very quietly, suddenly spoke out. "Sheila's right, we will, in the beginning, have to tread very carefully. Spirit obviously feel that as a group we will be able to get the message through to people in such a way—more direct than conventional method—but at the moment we desperately need experience working together so let's play it by ear. I suggest on Sunday that one of you open in prayer. I'll do the address then another can do the bible reading. Sheila can start off the clairvoyance and if any of us feel we have any message to give we'll do so at that time. What do you think?'' I nodded to Bill, as I looked around, noting that although no words were being spoken, I could tell the suggestion for the Sunday meeting had been approved.

After this discussion we then went into details of dress and decided to wear the same apparel as we had worn for the school demo. Sunday arrived all too soon, and we were travelling together in the one car. My brother, being a car salesman, was able usually to take a car of his choice from the showroom, therefore choosing one large enough to comfortably sit five people. We were all a little within our own thoughts—so making little remarks here and there, sometimes making an attempt at some small joke, which only produced a slight titter, being wasted due to the intense concentration of the approaching night's work ahead of us.

Breaking the silence I said to my brother, ''This must bring back memories to you—doesn't seem many months ago when you took Bill and I to this very same church. Strange that this should be our first to demonstrate in.'' He agreed, nodding his head. I couldn't see his face, sitting as I was in the back seat, but could tell the expression was one of wonder, for so little time had past since that night when I told him, ''You should be on a platform with us.''

I settled back comfortably in the car, thinking how beautifully things were going. I only hope that this was indeed what Spirit required of us. It was strange, I couldn't really see we were doing anything really different than the ordinary church meetings, only that there would be five instead of one or two workers. In those early days of the group many things seemed hard to understand, but it was evident that this was what Lucille, and our good friend, the doctor, wanted. Listening to those early tapes it was always spoken, time and time again, ''Five can work as one.'' I wonder—seems to me something will have to change before I can really understand the meaning of those words. Maybe tonight will be the answer. I closed my eyes, linking closely with my spirit helpers. ''We're in your hands,'' I said, ''If this is what you want of us then inspire us all to receive true, sincere communication, that we might receive the message of your intention.''

My sister-in-law's voice interrupted my inner thoughts. ''We're here,'' I think I heard her say as I pulled myself together the car gently slowing up. ''Yes, that's it,'' I smiled at her seeing the frightened look on her face. ''Don't worry,'' I said, encouragingly,

"It will be fine, you'll see." "I doubt it," she said, "I'm petrified. I won't get a thing, I know it. We should have waited for a time. I'm not ready to work." Her voice was now raised to a nervous edginess. "You'll be all right, we'll all be together, you'll not be on your own"—my husband was now trying to console her. "You see," he said, "It will be a piece of cake!"

I wasn't too sure I could agree with that statement—however, I refrained from saying so, as we walked into the church, being greeted, as was usual, by the chairman. "Now, what shall I introduce you as," she said, "Let's have your names, goodness that's going to take some introducing," as she wrote down the last name. "Maybe it would be better if I introduce you as Mrs. Macey and her group, that would be much easier." "Yes, that's fine," I said, having up until that moment not thought about the name of our group. We would have to think about that, the sooner the better, it's important to conduct ourselves with a little professionalism.

We had arrived fairly early, giving plenty of time to settle in our excited nerves. We found, on looking around, a couple of chairs on which us girls thankfully sat—the men standing around making light-hearted chatter to the chairman, who I could see was enjoying having three smart-looking males paying her so much attention. I, on the other hand, ignored the conversation and busied myself, taking stock of my surroundings. Although having been here a few times before, I am, by nature, a nosy sort of person, and I was taking note of the many objects of jumble which were still piled in one corner of the room. They did not appear to have been touched since our last visit, although I knew that this church, in particular, often had regular jumble sales. There was the old familiar rust-coloured chenille table cloth, showing worn patches, where probably, over many years, hot teapots had stood, leaving parts of it very threadbare. I could see from where I was sitting, right under the table, and by the thickness of its large oak legs, carved and shaped, this also had withstood much use in its past life, and still seemed to be doing a grand job.

At that moment a gentleman came in, struggling with a very large box, and dumped it, with relief, on to the table. "More gear for Saturday," he said. The chairlady was a little agitated at his untimely entrance, having by this time been completely weakened by the charm of the men around her, and was annoyed to have the pretty little scene disturbed so abruptly as we were each, in turn, introduced to the gentleman in question. I warmed immediately to his firm handshake, having not met him before, and liked his genuine interest as to the obvious change of service, which was apparent, seeing the five of us about to take the platform. We gave to him the only answer which could be given, "Wait and see, it's far too difficult to explain," we said. "I shall, with interest," he answered, and then left the room. After his exit it seemed so many different faces came in and out, some being introduced, others, possibly helpers of the church, less important, were not. Having by now set down the order of service, watches were synchronized, and the moment arrived, I, giving a friendly wink and good-luck sign to my sister-in-law as we made from our little room, taking the stairs which led on to the fine platform. Plenty of room for us all, I thought.

The service began and, as always, all was well once the link with Spirit was made, our contacts making direct communication. I was extremely pleased, when getting up to demonstrate clairvoyance, finding the other members of the group linking with me on the same message. This was surely unique, making the receiver of the message doubly sure of its spirit communicator. I don't think in all my experience, then or now, has there been a clairvoyance and demonstration of this nature. It was, to say the least, incredible. We finished the service, astounded at our own performance, little realizing at that stage that we had just begun a way of spirit communication, proving to others that the individual was unimportant. Spirit could, and would work, as a team, if only those on earth were prepared to stand down from their own pedestals and prove the teachings of love, in sharing and working together in harmony.

Leaving the church that night, I had no doubt as to how we were to work—that had now been shown, and with this knowledge I felt a wonderful glow within, knowing full well that we had been given a rare and truly powerful gift, and this was just the beginning. In time we would be able to give many great upliftments, for here, within our grasp, was a way of communication, giving accurate, without any doubt, proof of survival, in a way never demonstrated before. Five different individuals, working as one, a truly remarkable gift. To say we were uplifted with our efforts that night would be an understatement. We realised this was to be our future way of working, and on the way home we spoke with great enthusiasm, ready and eager to display this talent as often as the opportunity arose.

I had already decided to inform all future churches, where my husband and I would be working, that we would now be working as a group. I think it was that very night, on leaving the church, that the discussion arose about the naming of our group. What could we call ourselves? Each of us became very thoughtful, but did not make any hasty decision, preferring to wait for possible inspiration, which was to come a little later, a week or so after that evening, circle night, to be precise.

As usual we were discussing the instructions and teachings received from our guides, enjoying this time, relaxing together, each receiving warmth and love from one another. Those early days were so beautiful. We would retire into our lounge, a comfortable room. I had three large black swivel chairs which were indeed extremely comfortable, a large carpet, but not fitted, leaving the edges, which were parquet flooring, a very nice sideboard, which my husband had built, containing glassware and drink. I was very proud of that cabinet. We had an open coal fireplace, which is a rare sight today. I remember how Lady, our corgi, loved to lay in front of it, getting as close as she could possibly bear. Then there was the attractive looking lobster basket stool, made of cane, which I had got from saving my cigarette coupons. On the whole, quite a pleasant room. This, being where we would sit for many hours, discussing as always, the fascinating Spirit world.

I don't remember which one of us said it, but the idea came. How about using the initials of our surnames, being A.P.M. That was a possible suggestion, but didn't quite have the right ring to it. What about A.M.P. We all laughed, we would sound like some electric light company. There's always MAP Group, particularly as Lucille said that we would travel far and wide. Maybe MAP would be appropriate. We were all deeply thoughtful at this suggestion, but still did not feel in complete agreement. Then, as if by some unseen force, we looked at one another when we spelt out PAM. Why, that sounds good, the PAM Group, I repeated over and over again. We all responded our agreement, each happy with the new name, which was to be heard about, in those early days, far and wide, but of course to us at that time, unknown, probably unbelieving had we been told of our future progress.

We now began working every possible chance as a group. I was also approached by many women's clubs and political parties to give talks on spiritualism. So the group began to become well sought after, and on each demonstration we became stronger in links with one another. We were almost inseparable, when we weren't together we were in touch by phone, we were like the fingers of a hand, each as important as the other.

I found, during that time, the pressure of hospital life very demanding on me, possibly because we were living such a full life. Bringing up our children, running the home, plus the now much more demanding group, I knew that although I loved nursing it was having a very tiring effect on me, but was undecided as to whether to give in my notice of my intention to leave. I certainly loved hospital life, and had made many friends, but having to work on late duty really made the decision for me, and so I left. I felt very sad, feeling so much part of the hospital, and this was what I would miss most of all. I needed a rest before looking around for some other occupation for of course I could not afford to stay at home, due to financial demands, which were still a great pressure upon us, but a week or two was roughly about the time I would have had, for I remember how amazed I was when we were invited to the senior nursing officer's home, known in those days as the Matron, for a meal.

I had met her through a contact of an extremely sick nurse who had been in the ward I was working on. She had been suffering from exphilo dermotitis, a very unpleasant complaint. Her whole body was covered in ugly red blotches, her skin flaking like snow. I was given the duty to special her, which meant that I would take charge of her needs whilst on duty. It did not take much effort on my part to give her peace of mind, for I felt so confident that she would recover, even though medically her condition meant that she would suffer for many weeks. I told her that within a week her body would clear. I found the words were out before realizing it, just like I said, "I am a medium," many years ago when in the wages office. Only in this case there would be some sort of miracle. I arranged for my husband to make contact with her and, between the two of us, she did indeed regain her health within the time predicted, and because of the remarkable recovery, in her eyes, she had informed her friend who was a matron in another hospital. It was at her request that we made contact, and later became friends.

We were, this night, introduced to the superintendent of the domestics within the same hospital that I had just left. I was not sure what I was now going to do regarding work—the question being asked of me during the meal. I explained that after the exhilarating experience of hospital life I felt a little despondent at the thought of returning to office work, so I was astounded when asked if I would consider supervising domestics at the very same hospital which I had left only a few days before, the hours being considerably favourable and, financially, good. I there and then agreed, but hardly believing my good luck.

I found, to my satisfaction, that the change from nursing to supervising domestics, although completely different, was very enjoyable, still giving me the contacts already made, but now with less pressure. The group by this time, having established itself, took us to many places, and we found the possibility of helping the hospital in their forthcoming fete an enjoyable prospect. As always, there was terrific enthusiasm from the group. It was my brother's brilliant idea, as we wondered how we could raise money for the hospital, to approach a local business man whom he knew from his own profession, and who owned a genuine gypsy caravan. "I could have a word with him, maybe he will take it up to the hospital, for he also owns a fairground steam-organ, which indeed would also prove to be an attraction." My brother's voice was now very keen and anxious, knowing full well that these indeed would create a crowd—bringing with them the much needed public funds. "Oh, that sounds terrific," I cried, "Maybe if he lets us have the caravan we could dress up as gypsies, this really will bring in the crowds."

After being assured that permission had been granted the five of us made many plans for the approaching summer fete. We even included our young sons who seemed to like the idea of being bathed in brown make-up which we had bought from a theatrical shop. We made clothes for us girls, spotted scarves for the men and the boys, and on the day when we were all finally ready, we looked every bit authentic. I certainly didn't recognize myself with a black wig pulled back into a bun. I really looked an old woman, my sister-in-law looking quite the reverse, rather pretty—also wearing a black wig, but hanging down one side in a long ringlet, which gave her an extremely attractive look. The colours of us all were of course, outstanding. I shall never forget the stares we received as we travelled by car to the hospital. Some even pressed their horns in appreciation of our obvious, gay and happy, attraction.

On arriving at the hospital, once being seen by the owner of this truly magnificent caravan, permission was granted for me to actually sit inside and give crystal ball readings. These were hilarious, for I was using a glass ball taken from a fisherman's net. This was carefully placed on a small box, which we had draped in black velvet, knowing full well that it would be a crowd puller. We had also put up a tent next to the van where Keith and Bill could also give readings, charging half-a-crown for their services and three-and-sixpence if they preferred to come in to the caravan. My brother, who was very musically talented, brought his accordian along, and he and his wife, and the children, were in charge of the money, also taking care of the public by playing tunes and singing together. On the whole a truly colourful, happy and well-turned out side show.

One thing stands out clearly in my mind, and never fails to make me laugh. We had attracted quite a queue for readings to be told, and a little old lady was helped into the caravan. She sat nervously down and I proceeded to tell her so-called fortune, through the eye of the crystal ball, but of course, I was really linking with spirit. I told her quite a few things, and then said, "Do mind your legs, take care where steps are concerned, I see you falling." She thanked me and left the tiny caravan, promptly falling down the steps. When my brother quickly picked her up, she turned round to the large crowd who were waiting, saying, "Good God, she's good, she just told me to watch my step." Well, on hearing this I nearly collapsed, and found great difficulty in composing myself for the next client.

I think, in all, we made for the hospital about £30. Which was an awful lot of readings. We were completely exhausted, but deeply satisfied with our efforts. Let me add, it took days before we finally got rid of the liquid make-up, but it was all worthwhile, although I can remember, if I am honest, on feeling a little disappointed a few days later, on standing at the bus stop, seeing we had made front page news in the local rag—a beautiful picture of us all—but nobody could recognize us.

So many different opportunities seemed to be coming our way, and we were always keen to get involved, displaying our talents, eager to demonstrate. The PAM group was now becoming, within the spiritualist movement, a recognizable name. This was apparent on our appearance at the annual *Psychic News* Dinner and Dance, having the photographer anxious to take our picture, and a reporter also taking particulars, both of which would be amongst the other well-known mediums' articles, due to be in that publication, following their attendance at that night's events.

I do believe that was the start of things turning sour. For as soon as the PAM group made news within the movement, it was only small things, but noticably catty and unfriendly remarks, that eventually came back to us. This we found hurtful, and a little astonishing, having until then met only with sincerity, but having so much strength and the confidence that what we were doing was a wonderful way of bringing the movement out of hidden doors, showing through us a light modern approach, and an attractive manner, we knew we were on the right lines.

Our mode of dress was, to say the least, a little outstanding, possibly giving the impression of being on a stage rather than a church platform. The men wore black dinner-suits, white shirts and black velvet ties, and the two ladies, looking equally attractive, wore long black skirts and white blouses. I remember reading one press cutting quoting, "They resemble a dance band." Maybe we did, to us it was a kind of uniform in dressing this way. There could be no distraction that one may look better than the other, therefore giving close harmony, feeling each as good and looking identical, played for us, an important part within the group.

So ignoring many harsh words against us, we carried the group further into the public eye. We opened a spiritualist church simply by hiring a local Co-op hall, and through advertising was able to bring many members of the public to regular weekly meetings. This was even carried out a little differently to the conventional methods.

Every other week we would conduct an evening of questions and answers, spending the whole of the time on this, not just a little while after the service, which many churches would do. The need was very apparent to us, for the congregation was always larger on these nights. We gained a great deal of knowledge, for we engaged many workers, and it was good to share points of view.

I look back with affection and happy memories of the Co-op hall. We had been given an old church organ, permission being granted for us to leave it at the hall, having up until then been using tape-recorded music for the hymns. It was a great moment, the Monday we were able, through the talents of my brother, to have live music for us all to sing to. Because of the position of the hall the only place the organ could stand was behind the congregation. That didn't seem to be a problem although I can recall that it was a little noisy, for being so old, much energy was needed to pump the pedals, allowing the sound of my brother's feet going up and down to travel, but like the bag-pipes, once blown, beautiful music was created.

The people arrived and all too soon the service began, my dear brother seated majestically, played the introduction of *All Things Bright and Beautiful.* I gave an encouraging wink of approval as the congregation stood up, and we all sang with great gusto, mostly to disguise the noise of the bellows. I, being on the platform, was facing this wonderful work of art and sang even louder. My brother's voice could now be heard, loud, completely unaware of what was happening to him, as his feet were pounding up and down, his hands banging out the notes. By this time the people were swaying, singing their hearts out, myself included, when, in astonishment, I noticed the chair he was sitting on was gradually leaving the organ and his body was getting further and further away—thus making a very comic figure—arms now outstretched trying to continue, the congregation singing *The Lord God Made Them All,* unaware of the drama that was going on behind them, and there were still two verses to go.

How I controlled my strong desire to laugh I shall never know, when having by this time stretched himself like a piece of elastic, and managed through Bill, seeing his predicament, to get the chair back in order—was able to complete the hymn, sweat pouring from him. That must have been the hardest performance of his life, and he made sure that he was not going to experience such an embarrassment again, for he always tied his chair to the organ after that night.

We learned an awful lot, having the responsibility of running this church, it also gave us opportunities to try many new things. We encouraged other working mediums, also giving them a free hand, and many an enjoyable evening was spent. The main object was to encourage sharing, whatever the gift, and many were surprised by our views and more than pleased when given a free hand to demonstrate their gifts of healing, even though we ourselves gave healing after every meeting. Even now, I don't think this is encouraged, for it is part of the church, and the presidents and members their job, and their helpers, and outsiders would not be encouraged to use their gifts. However, this was our way, sharing together, getting away from the individual.

We still continued our little circle, as often as time would allow, and were taught the importance of doing so, rather than alone, and still dear Lucille would remind us that we must not change—don't let others change you—be as you are—you will go far. Her words were repeated so many, many times.

It was jolly hard sometimes trying to be ourselves. Being in the public eye did give us a feeling of importance, but we tried in the beginning not to let the publicity interfere with what we were, but it was becoming noticeable—how we thrived on being noticed. Maybe a perfectly natural reaction, but it seemed at the time most important, and we were more than a little put out if, on arriving at a new church, were not immediately recognised, We, of course, would not admit this to one another, but continued on, doing our best wherever we went.

We also kept our little Co-op hall, giving others the responsibility of keeping it running smoothly when we were away working. We continued this for quite some time until, much to our distress, the hall was needed for evening classes. We were offered a room at the top of the building, which had we accepted, would have lost us many of our older friends, due to their inability in climbing the many stairs, and so, with sadness, we closed our little weekly meeting at the Co-op.

We continued working, finding special nights were becoming far more popular. Churches found they could increase their revenue, having five upon their platform, and many let us also demonstrate healing, making an interesting evening and therefore filling the churches. We also did have the opportunity of demonstrating our gift at the Enfield Church, to which the chairman had invited us, quite a long time ago when at the school hall. We were also travelling long distances, coming home tired and sometimes exhausted, but we were happy, enjoying to the full the limelight we were getting. We still continued to have circle as often as our work would allow, and we were encouraged to take our demonstrations outside of the churches, hiring our own halls, getting to non-spiritualists.

Now this was very hard work, also expensive. There was the hiring first, which we had agreed should be, if possible, town halls, usually the reason being easy to get at, always on bus routes, and railway stations often very near, Then there would be the expense of advertising. We dispensed with tickets, having learnt from past mistakes, better to pay at the door, the hard work of having posters, advertising the event, begging most local shops to display them in their windows—then the demonstration itself, working amongst 90% non-spiritualists, to put it bluntly, took guts, and we certainly had plenty of that. At the end of this we invariably would be out of pocket, but it didn't matter. We felt we were doing a very necessary job, spreading the word, and always before doing such a demonstration, checked where the local spiritualist church was. So on the many enquiries, after a successful evening, we could refer them to find out more from their local church in the area.

We must have been to many town halls over a certain period of time, but because of the intense pressure, and lack of funds, put it aside, agreeing that later we would explore this nature of working more fully. It was a relief at that time, for the PAM group seemed to be working almost week in and week out, travelling great distances. A very well-known medium who lived in Scotland heard about us, and we were grateful to him, for although he had not seen us work, he spread the group's name wherever he went, and often I would receive a letter from a church requesting a booking on the recommendation of his name. It was quite sometime before we finally got to meet him, and were able to thank him for his help, and on the first meeting he asked us if we would be prepared to travel to Scotland on tour and work the many churches that they have there. We were completely bowled over by this, thrilled at the opportunity, and deeply grateful to him.

This took some time to organise, but we decided on our annual holiday, the first week in September. What a bonus, we thought, going on tour. We must be good, feeling a little more over-confident, although we would not have admitted it. I knew we were aware, it showed in our attitude, not from the platform, but definitely behind the scenes. I was no different from the rest, thriving on any publicity which might come our way. I did notice, however, that we had changed. There did not seem to be the fun together as we used to have, there was also criticism amongst ourselves—sometimes this became out of hand, which caused bad feelings. Keith was becoming much more agitated, he did have domestic problems, and the now much sought-after group caused, for him, difficulties in making the many meetings, which created lack of understanding towards him, the feeling being that the group must come first at all times, regardless, so it was not such a shock to us that he decided to resign from the group.

It was not easy at first, I felt his absence quite strongly, although not having to make excuses for him, did make life within the group much happier. Keith made his departure from us two weeks before we went on tour, so it was only now the four of us. I did not think our performance would be too much noticeably different, for working, as we did, one would not be missed, but the physical impact hit us all at first, for we did feel the loss, as I am sure Keith must have done.

That first tour gave to us much valuable experience. We found the Scottish people receptive to our way of working, the president, and members of the churches, showing us hospitality to which we had not been accustomed in the many places we had worked back home. Here we were made to feel very welcome, not only in their churches, but also in their private homes. Thinking back, it could not have been easy, accommodating four people, and we were appreciative to their efforts. To say we were exhausted at the end of the week was absolutely true. We had driven over a thousand miles, ending up the last night in Liverpool, looking very tired, but knowing that we could not relax until after the evening's demonstration, which we did, and found to our surprise, although physically tired, very satisfying. We had gained on our first tour valuable experience, necessary to the future success of the group.

It took us time to settle on returning home, having now tasted the excitement of being away on tour. We had also gained press recognition, which at the time was important to us. We discussed between us every meeting, reliving each demonstration. sometimes quite cruelly if one of us had not, within the eyes of the others, performed as well, or perhaps stolen the limelight, from the other three. I always hated this—a bit like a post-mortem—but we felt it was imperative to the group's future success, which, on looking back, added only more aggravation amongst us.

Church bookings came in thick and fast, filling our diaries, until we had to draw a halt when we found we had bookings for two years in advance. It seemed at the time spiritualism had taken hold, leaving us very little time for our own personal life, going out as often as we did, weekdays, week-ends, every moment of our spare time was taken giving demonstrations. Slowly changing us, certainly not noticeable, apart from our obvious presentation, which was very professional, due to our many public meetings, but I could feel certain changes. I used to shake it off, not wanting to be aware, and tried desparately to ignore these feelings.

We attracted so many young people as followers, and we found that we could relate to them without any difficulty. A well-known young healer, had about this time, contacted us, having an idea in putting on a very large meeting and wondered if we would consider sharing the platform with him, using our mediumship and experience gained from the many outside meetings that we had already done. The area suggested was Leeds Town Hall.

This needed a great deal of organisation, we would also be required to split the expenses, and we weren't dealing now in pennies. We spent many hours in this young gentleman's company, discussing all aspects of the proposed venue. We made contact with the late Fred Moore, a very well-known and highly respected figure in the movement, who was extremely helpful, not only for his expertise in the organization of large meetings, but he had the added advantage of living a stone's throw away from the town hall, and he was also able to supply us with the necessary literature. Having access to his own christian spiritualist press, he offered to send forthcoming notices of our demonstration to all the churches within the Leeds area.

It was important for us to make physical contact, having dealt with many matters over the telephone, and we were expected to meet an official of the town hall in person and discuss with him the nature of our requirements. This was no ordinary small hall that we were booking, so we made arrangements to make a detour on our way home from a northern tour that we had just completed. Tired and hungry, we found ourselves looking around this magnificent building, a fine piece of architecture, so old and yet so graceful. The size was gigantic, one felt very small inside the banqueting hall. To believe that our intention was to work upon its rostrum was to believe we were going to be invaded by spacemen. It seemed so far-fetched, the cost alone had got to be a fortune, I thought, as our footsteps could be heard echoing inside the vast hall.

Somehow it was going to work, we signed our names to a couple of forms, agreeing on a date of venue, and like being in some sort of trance, shook hands with the town clerk, and left, looking back at the great oak door with awe—shakily climbing down the marble steps, finding the nearest coffee bar, where we could catch our breath, and talk over what we had just committed ourselves to. The cost was astronomical, but there were to be six of us in all, so on dividing the amount it did look a little more realistic.

We explored the area and left a few posters in local shops, then a visit to the local press office, securing advertisements to be inserted weekly, one month before the now approved date. This was a very large hall, and we would require something like over a thousand people if the venture was to be worthwhile. The very thought of the whole thing gave me many sleepless nights. I kept wondering, were we ready for something as large as this.

The young healer was very enthusiastic and did not seem in the least bit nervous, as he arranged with another young fellow what they had in mind, unaware, or least appeared unaware, of our nervousness—showing little nervousness himself as the day grew nearer. I kept seeing in my mind's eye that school hall many years earlier, those rows and rows of empty chairs. What if the same thing happened, what would we do, it just didn't bear thinking about, but I couldn't, no matter how I tried, have the confidence that we could fill that great hall. It was enormous, and looked even larger in the imagination of my mind. I had visions of the great chandeliers blaring down their expanse of light, picking out like a spotlight one or two, and our group having to be part of the audience to allow our friends to demonstrate the power of healing, and then quickly changing over so we, as a group, could have at least someone, each to give our clairvoyance.

Oh ye of little faith, I could hear my conscience accuse me. I'm jolly sure the rest were feeling just the same, but weren't letting on. You could tell, as the day grew nearer, the usual tell-tale nervousness, an uncontrollable dry cough, odd bursts of forced laughter—they may have been fooling others, but not me—we were so scared. Had we some way of getting out we would have escaped, but we were in it right up to our necks.

So when the day did arrive, it was more relief just to get it over with than anything else. It was a long journey to Yorkshire, and the day was none to bright—rather cold and wet. Still, we started very early, there was plenty of time for the weather to change. A wet night would not enhance the evening, so as we travelled on that long journey, feeling very apprehensive, deep within our own thoughts, wondering how our two young friends were, and if they also had left home and started on their way. We hoped to arrive just after lunch, giving us a few hours before having to face the ordeal. I suppose, looking back, that was the biggest public thing we ever had to face. We reached the town in good time, checked all was well with our advertising, noticing that many local shops were displaying our posters, which looked very impressive in bold lettering. Leeds Town Hall seemed to jump out, giving a 3-D view.

The evening came all too quickly. We were escorted behind the vast stage, and then we concentrated in getting ourselves ready. My sister-in-law's hem had come undone on her skirt. This did not help in keeping us calm, only gave us more things to worry about. However, a needle was magically produced and hastily I repaired the offending hem. We had a few well-wishers, who came from quite a distance to wish us luck. At one time the dressing-room became so crowded it made one feel like a bunch of actors waiting for the curtain to rise. Little bits of information kept coming, boosting our morale, like, "There's quite a queue outside, goes right round the corner."

But the moment we stepped on to that stage I knew we had made it. There had to be at least a thousand people, all that ground work had not been wasted, all those past weeks of planning had, to our astonishment materialized. The people had come, now it was up to us to give them proof of survival, which we did, giving of our best in the only way the PAM group could, pure, simple, and above all, sincere—working as a team in unity, loving our work and showing to those that watched our very close links together. Our love of Spirit shone, making the onlooker see us differently to any other kind of medium worker seen before.

Yes, the night was successful, our friends received good results with the healing, and I believe we added another large piece of experience to our now rather powerful group, bringing with it a little more egotism. We were asked to take over a small church in Enfield, which had been going on for many years, but its congregation had dwindled to practically none. The president had contacted us, having already seen the success we had had in the small Co-op hall, and asked if we would be prepared to take it over for him, rather than close it.

This was for us a great challenge so we accepted on the condition that we ran it for one year only, for we had future plans for the group which did not include being tied to one particular church. We had handbills printed, and one free week-end we distributed them, one by one, in nearly every house in the vicinity of the church. This, I remember, was very heavy going on the feet. We must have walked miles, but it was worthwhile seeing so many faces the first night we demonstrated, giving the president great upliftment to see such an unusually full gathering, taking him completely by surprise, although justifying his approach to us in saving the little church—also paying back some of the money already paid out in the hiring of the small hall, where this church had been run for so many years. We now had this responsibility, on top of our over-full programme, but somehow we managed, enjoying helping where we could, newcomers to the movement.

My sister-in-law now joined me at the hospital, having accepted a vacancy which had become open in the domestic supervisory department. It was nice having her with me during the day, and it also gave us both a chance to discuss things which possibly were on our minds, but found difficulty to put into words when we were all together. I enjoyed these times and would not have thought possible, a few years later, that yet again history would repeat itself and our relationship would come to a spiritual end.

So much was happening, invitations came our way, we met people, and being so much in demand, gave us a feeling of grandeur—although I don't think we would have admitted to that.

I knew I caused problems on meeting certain people, those a little out of our class. I never felt comfortable with them although I was equipped with enough intelligence and table manners to mix with the best. To me, personally I knew where I was best, amongst my own class. Never let it be said that the middle classes are a thing of the past. I would, by experience, beg to differ. They did exist and still do. That would always be part of our British heritage. They are usually awfully nice, and sometimes charming people, but not for me or my husband.

This caused a little misunderstanding, for my brother enjoyed mixing with those, to put the expression mildly, above his class and that of his wife. This sometimes caused a split between us, they having become very friendly with an influential lady who gave many dinner parties, to which, of course, the group were given invites. After one or two, however, I found them not to my taste, not only did I find it all a little false putting on certain airs, my stomach also could not take the very rich food, rejecting it with shock, having until then been only accustomed to good plain cooking.

We did not think at the time that perhaps it was wrong for us not to continue to stay as a group on these occasions, because we had all agreed previously that we should have our own friends and outside interests, just as long as we were together for spiritual work. Gradually, over a year or so, we began to see less of one another. I also found that the domestic side of hospital life was not really me, so I left and went back into office work, at first settling in an engineering firm, gaining experience, until the opportunity came for me to be accepted into local government, where I stayed for many years.

We still worked really hard as a group, finding stiff opposition from those who found our style of work not to their liking, but we were determined to carry on as we knew that what we had was indeed worth persevering with, no matter how difficult and annoying. So we continued in strength from the rostrum—we displayed four very happy people, working together in perfect harmony. If only it could have continued on, but something was going radically wrong. I couldn't put my finger on it—just small things at first, like our dress, which, as I explained earlier, was identical even to our jewellery—simple little necklaces. I noticed my sister-in-law was beginning to wear very different pieces, which gave me the feeling that she was wanting to be known as an individual. I never approached her on this thinking to myself that perhaps I was being a little too silly over the matter, so shrugged it off not wanting to cause disharmony, hoping that everything would right itself with the tour, which was coming up in Wales.

We were to share a large caravan together as a base and travel from there to the various churches on the programme. This, I thought, would give us the chance of getting closer together. As it turned out, having six days together was fun, just like the old days, and was like an answer to a prayer. "Please," I said, over and over again, "Let us save what we have." I couldn't bear the thought of the group's split.

We found the caravan very tastefully furnished and there was plenty of room for us all. The day we arrived was the only spare-time we had for each evening was booked. So after unpacking we did a little sightseeing, getting back in time to dress and travel to the various churches on tour. The main thing was, we were together, and able to discuss each meeting, either the same evening or after breakfast the next day.

All went well, until one rather unhappy meeting—perhaps we were not on form, maybe tired, one could blame it on to the congregation—they possibly were not responsive to our manner of work. I do believe it was us, no excuse—the night was a disaster. It seemed nothing would be accepted, whatever was said the response was no they couldn't take our message, leaving us very fraught and frustrated—leaving a nasty taste on our ego—this couldn't be happening to us. "Ah well, never mind, it happens to everyone sometime or another," I said, as we left the church, but it wasn't left.

On returning home to the caravan, after settling down with another coffee, like a tornado harsh words were said. I couldn't believe that after all those years, working together, growing stronger, that we were capable of arguing with one another. Surely we had advanced more spiritually than that! Many unkind things were said, cruel criticism, the warning I had received a month earlier was now becoming apparent to me. I never said a lot that night, but knew in my heart that this was to be our last tour together, although I kept these thoughts very much to myself.

When Bill and I finally, at the end of the week were back in our own home, I cried deeply to him. I was truly shaken by the attack and needed much strength to continue working with the group. Luckily things were a little slack regarding church bookings, so when we did meet together it was not so frequent. The little church had managed to keep its now much larger congregation, and the group took turns on being there on Sundays. My brother and his wife one week, Bill and I on the alternative weeks. These meetings were always a joy, giving opportunity to new mediums who wished to do platform work. Our church was always open to them. It was hard to believe we had completed the year, and we left, leaving a very happy gathering there. I wonder now if that little church is still going. One day I shall have to investigate and see.

Now being released from the church more time was available to us. For some reason our group demonstrations, although booked for two years in advance, certainly were well spaced out, sometimes as long as six or eight weeks between them, and yet when coming together on the platform we still gave an impression of unity and love. Many would come up to us and say how they envied our closeness to one another. The pretence was becoming for me artificial, and after much heartache I decided that unless we could, do something about the barrier between us, then I could not endure it any longer—to me we were being hypocritical.

We had a long discussion where I tried very hard—"Could we not be as we were, as one, close, enjoying each other's company as we had done in the past," I said. Surely we were putting on a false impression to others. We did not socialize any more together. My point was not understood, they could not see what I was seeing—perhaps others had changed their views, and so yet again something which I loved dearly was falling apart, and I could do nothing to save it.

The years we spent as a group, I shall never regret. It was, and could have been a most wonderful spiritual gift, and what we had no one has ever been able to copy, four mediums working as one, spiritualism had within their grasp a propaganda group stronger than it will ever have again. It's now just a memory.

CHAPTER FOUR

NEARER MY GOD TO THEE

Getting up the next day after the disbanding of the group, I felt strangely different. I shook myself—it's only natural—one could not, after such a long time, forget the experience that we had just been through. I filled the electric kettle up—once I've had some coffee I shall probably feel better. How I wished that I could make an excuse not to go into work, but I did hold a responsible position and my absence would only cause more confusion for me when I returned. I made my coffee and sat heavily down. How I longed for someone to talk to. I sipped the coffee—what had I done—did I do right—my finger making circles on the rim of the mug as I thoughtfully sat staring into space. I knew any minute I would have to move. I looked upon the beautiful wall clock and saw the time drawing nearer—urging me that I would miss my train. I gazed at it—how clever to have designed the signs of the Zodiac. I focused my eyes on the doublehead of the twin, that's me! I certainly lived up to the sign. I suddenly became aware, on looking up at the clock, that on either side of my sign was the Bull and the Crab, and a meaning seemed to strike me. I was being charged on by the bull and, at this very moment, I was skuttling away like a crab. No, this must not do—things must not stop now. I must continue on.

I then decided that I had now taken far too long, and hurriedly left the house, but feeling more confident than half-an-hour or so before. On returning home that night I made a point of being particularly cheerful—for I knew my husband was more than a little upset. He had such great plans for the group and he tried much more than I to keep us together. Often, between the long gaps at meetings, he would pop out on a Sunday morning on the pretence of getting a newspaper, but really his intention was to visit my brother's house trying his best to keep a closer link between us—and they, being so unaware of the ever-increasing wide gap that was so evident.

Never mind—I suppose one would put it all down to experience. I do hope that we did learn from the adventure otherwise all those years of working together—the many tears shed, the hard criticism we had to bear, surely was for some purpose! Bill was, as I already guessed, a little downhearted when he came into the little room which for many years had served as a circle and healing room. Now, because we were on our own, we had turned one of the bedrooms into a seance room.

It was decorated in a modern design and because it contained a dinette suite—we used it for our meals. I quickly put his dinner on the table—making light conversation. As he changed his shoes—"Had a good day?" I said. "Not bad," came back the answer. "How about you?" He came out to me in the kitchen, giving me, as always, a hug and a kiss. "Bit of a bore," I said, "Still we're home now, let's not talk about work."

Bill agreed and sat himself down at the table—scrutinising the meal which was in front of him. "This looks different—what is it?" "Oh, something new they've come out with. Being a working girl the frozen food companies certainly did well out of me—for I spent as little time as possible at the cooker, not wanting to waste any precious time. "Seems sort of strange doesn't it," I said, "I do feel somehow released." Bill looked at me thoughtfully, "It was only a matter of time before something happened," he said.

I nodded, turning my fork amongst the food—playing with it—I didn't have much of an appetite. "I wonder why! We did so well together." I wasn't really speaking to Bill—just more-or-less talking and answering myself. "Do you think I did the right thing—I mean breaking it so soon? Should I have left it a little? Quite honestly, Bill, I could not have taken the strain much longer—but was I wrong," I asked him earnestly. "Look love, you most of all gave your all in keeping us together—others came in and influenced causing disharmony—you have only got to look back to the many so-called friends, whom we ignored, saying to us that we would be better to work on our own. Knowing the many jealousies around the group was something for many workers to be afraid of especially our growing popularity."

"Lucille has warned us of that many times—yet still outside

influence was allowed to creep in. A great pity, but you did do right. We were not any longer a group of unity—yet spirit stood by at every public demonstration not letting us down—knowing full well the strain we were under up to the last, and we managed without giving one hint to the public of the growing distance amongst us.'' My husband's words were taking effect. I began to feel a little easier. "Yes, you're right dear.'' I pushed the plate away—although I had eaten most of it, it did nothing apart from fill an empty hole—for it had been some hours since I had last eaten. I was now very figure conscious and was no more the glutton of past years. I had educated my stomach and although slightly on the tubby side, I was at least a stone and a half lighter and now tipped the scales between nine and a half to just under ten stone, depending on my diet. As long as I could continue to wear a size fourteen then I was happy.

Bill made the coffee whilst I washed up. We then went into the lounge and both settled comfortably in the armchairs, I tucking my legs under me—much easier to do than in the old black swivel chairs we used to have. We never bothered switching the television on, but just relaxed—enjoying the peace—having both an hour or so ago been amongst the ever increasing noise of the working world. It was good just sitting there saying nothing—shaking the day's events from us.

After about ten minutes, in fact I could feel myself beginning to nod, Bill spoke, bringing me back quickly to my senses. "Once you have written to all the churches cancelling the group's demonstrations, I think it best that we try to forget the past few years—let's concentrate on the future. I'm sure there's still much more ahead for us both—there's the physical circle for a start. Look what good results we have received so far. There is no telling what we will find in the future—now we can give more of ourselves than before.'' I nodded in agreement—the circle did appear to be very exciting. We had been interested in this for some time and had been sitting now for just about six months—having advertised for experienced sitters in the *Psychic News*. The group had discussed this a few years earlier, but only after careful thinking did we decide to actually start one. But not as I had hoped, altogether. My brother and his wife preferred to begin one of their own, believing that this might be good for their own experience—which made good sense—and I believe were getting good results. As to our own—it was becoming very interesting.

So I did just what my husband advised—brought myself together—and wrote to the many churches cancelling the group's engagements—those words reminding me vividly, "It is with regret the PAM group has now disbanded, etc. . ."

Now I felt, having no other pressure upon us, I could give myself without worry or depletion to my own physical strength. Bill, from the start, found the circle full of fascination seeing with his own eyes many things which he wanted, above all, to capture on film for me to see. So being an amateur photographer he read a great deal about infra-red film and experimented as often as he could. Many times, greatly disappointed, nothing developed. Never mind, I would say, next time perhaps. He would dig deeper into his photography magazines trying to find the answer. This kept him amused and also helped him to adjust from the hectic life to the now comparative calm.

It was felt that the time was ready for a cabinet to be built and this was done ingeniously. My husband could be, at times, so very clever. He made a framework of wood to represent the back and two door sides—covering them each in black taffeta. He drilled holes to the bottom and tops of them all—then with small nuts and bolts could assemble the three pieces together. A small wooden roof was then fixed on to the top and to complete the box a railing rod containing a black curtain fitted snuggly on to hooks on either side. Thus, when not in use, could be folded down easily to fit against one of our bedroom walls—not taking up much space at all—although space was not so important to us now—having seen both the children nicely settled into marriage.

At first the house seemed so empty—having over a number of years not only entertained our own guests, but constantly being invaded with many teenagers. Our children, knowing no other way of life, having mediums as parents, accepted our way quite naturally—although we took care not to encourage them for, like us, we wanted them to find it in their own way. We took great care not to influence them and allowed them to grow up finding out for themselves—when they were good and ready, and of course having such an upbringing it is not so surprising that they both are very spiritually minded and often contact us when they have any important decisions to make in order that we might be able to give them spirit advice.

I smile to myself—looking back to when my daughter was quite young. One particular day she had deliberately told us a lie and we had chastised her. She looked at us, tears rolling down her face—it's not fair—my friends can tell lies and their parents believe them—why should I have to have a mother and father who can see right through me—her little face really cross with us. We laugh about that when we are together—now we have a lovely relationship and are able to converse without any difficulty—although at times my husband and daughter are not always on the same wavelength. Where healing is concerned, for she is a qualified nurse and is inclined to be more scientific, she naturally accepts the medical side to be more beneficial—although she can be tied into knots on the many cases which have been spiritually cured and will admit, having seen through the years, the remarkable and sometimes miraculous cures. She usually gives in gracefully, saying O.K. dad, you win!

I must admit to being a typical parent—very proud of the way our children have turned out—for in the early days they had it pretty hard, but came through it all unscathed. Yes, we had much to be thankful for, and it will be a great thrill when our son follows his father's footsteps into healing—which I can see will happen. The gift is very prominent with him although he does not practise it. I do believe he is aware and, in the not too distant future, I shall not be surprised to see him turn towards the spiritual pathway—which we, so many years before, had taken.

Our own experience over many years had taught us much, but we knew there was still a lot to learn. We were still at the tip of the iceberg—so many different avenues to explore—and would not accept anything readily—being the first to analyse every new spiritual experience. Therefore, the physical circle gave much for us to investigate and we were not going to accept—even though conducted in our own home—on face value.

The cabinet, now completed, was placed inside the room and a small armchair was held within—the purpose being for me to sit inside the closed cabinet—putting myself into a trance condition and, hopefully, encourage through the love and energy of the sitters, physical phenomena. This could be very exhausting, for certain vibrations were needed in creating and attracting a powerful build up that Spirit could use which would eventually produce the phenomena.

We had ten sitters, including myself, who in dedication, would sing their very hearts out—hoping with their efforts to build the vibrations—and listening to some of those tapes I'd be inclined not to want to make contact. The noise was unbelievable! I have often wondered what the neighbours thought, but have never received any complaints—just at times, odd looks. Every week we sat, hoping that we were giving the right vibrations. In this manner it did seem the more light-hearted the sitters were—Spirit made more positive contact—and so it was not unusual to have old-time musical songs being sung.

Within a short time direct voice was evident, coming mostly from the direction of the ceiling—a young child known as Sally-Ann made herself known to us and became a very regular visitor—giving us all sorts of information about the Spirit world. I must have literally dozens of tapes of her sweet little voice. I became more used to being enclosed inside the cabinet and it was obvious this was indeed required if we were to receive definite Spirit contact.

Bill would set his camera on its tripod—religiously every week—ready should the opportunity of a Spirit visitation show itself. He was not to be disappointed. We do have exceptional photographs, but I feel, as he does, that we are still investigating and it is far better, at this stage, not to try to convince sceptics—as so many of the movement try to do. So better to wait—no matter how long—providing when the evidence comes it will be so evidential. Even then, I personally think, that having found a remarkable contact within another world, it is not really necessary to prove—surely proof for oneself is the most important.

I speak of how I feel deep within—while we have the material around us it cannot fail to show its greed. So much has happened. I have seen and talked, with so many people—in all walks of life—no one will change how I feel about Spirit, but now I can be myself I don't have to put on any act. If people want proof of survival—then I'm here to give them that—but behind the scenes—that way I can be sure of my own sincerity. True, over the many years we are quite well known, but to those who know us personally, we do try not to give any impression of being in anyway different. We have always tried to keep our feet firmly on the ground and do not encourage anything or anybody who tries to make Spirit out as something that it is not. I must have met, without exaggeration, hundreds of misguided people—sadly, many within the spiritualist movement—who seem to allow themselves to think that Spirit is some sort of weird powerful hidden phenomena and can, at will, take over one's soul—giving sadly to the enquiry—oddity and ridicule. To them, I say, wake up—be realistic—you are living in a dream world. To the many like myself, I would say, never stop searching—so much is yet still to be shown.

The hours my husband and I have sat together discussing over and over again the many aspects of Spirit and have never, as yet, come to the point of being bored with the conversation. Twice a week our home is filled with people—some seeking healing—others who come just to be with those who care—perhaps on the pretence of healing—it doesn't matter—they can experience a little of what we have found. I have changed a great deal in a lot of ways—possibly due to the different situations that have happened over the past couple of years. Maybe one would say I've grown up! Perhaps I have had my head in the clouds for too long!

The physical circle had given me much to think about. I can understand the power of thought—how powerful this can be. I have noticed a change in my husband—he is much more positive in his contact with Spirit and has found that he can go deep within himself—receiving sometimes quite brilliant inspirations—of which we both receive advantage by drawing from its power. I have also learnt it is all too easy to criticize others, but until one can look into oneself and see one's faults—our aim should be to look instead for the finer qualities, which we all possess somewhere within our make-up.

The word "understanding" is, in my view, very much underrated. To me it's one of the hardest words in our vocabulary, not to pronounce, but to act upon. Let me show an example, if I can—amongst the sitters in my circle was a lady who lost, through a road accident, her only child at the age of twenty-one. Tragic one would say—her obvious interest in the physical circle was to see her daughter materialize—we all wanted this so badly for her, but during the three to four years that she patiently sat—apart from small indications of her daughter's existence, materialization for her was not forthcoming—and so she became a little bitter—stating more or less at each circle night—that it would not be her luck to see her loved one—the rest of the sitters became impatient with her, therefore causing slight disharmony.

I would have given the world to have produced this Spirit for her—and yet even I would come before circle a little annoyed. I never, like the rest, truly understood her feelings. Each one's loss is different to the other—and being as the passing was at least some years' back, I did not understand her measure of grief. Her sister and brother-in-law would come each week hoping and praying, but they also seemed to feel this bitterness—without realizing that they were only creating some sort of barrier. They left eventually, not finding what they were dearly looking for. The sense of relief amongst the sitters on their departure was clearly shown. But looking back, did we understand! I don't think we did. I hope, should those dear friends read this story, know that at least they have the consolation that the circle was not meant for spectacular Spirit forms. I have no doubt that in time, with the right atmosphere, that loved one would have appeared.

How can we change us. We can't—only try to see others—which is not at all easy. I become, at times, frustrated—because others are perhaps not as dedicated to Spirit—choosing both worlds—Spirit being very much a hobby rather than a way of life. So often do I hear "O.K., providing it doesn't interfere with my material life"—and on the defensive would say, "I have to live Spirit—it must fit in, but not intrude"—and yet are only too happy to accept the many wonderful messages and upliftment when they are at their lowest ebb. But that word "understanding" creeps in. Who am I to decry others? What my husband and I do and how we act is our business—and if we choose to work so much with Spirit—that's up to us, and we should not expect so much of others—just encourage them during the time they are with us—whether it be a day or a year.

People and their religions can be strong. Some ready and willing—sometimes much to gullible—accepting every word given to them—others completely the reverse—not wanting anything to do with life hereafter—so-called death. This struck me as very clear when after a circle I was told that the filmstar, Michael Wilding, was wanting to speak to a well-known gentleman on Earth—and could we possibly get in touch with him. He said, "If you do, please let him know 'the door is now open,' and I will contact you again." Well, I did as I was asked of me—and was able to speak to the gentleman in question, who told me that although he was indeed quite shocked that Michael Wilding should want to speak to him—he did admit that in the early years they were quite close, but lost contact. I gave him the tiny message—saying that he would possibly make contact again—and could I, if necessary, get in touch with him—his answer being a definite, "No thank you."

A few weeks after this encounter it was not surprising to see this very man on a well-known show—whose star entertainer opened a door—and there he stood. I doubt very much if he realised that was what Michael Wilding was trying to tell him—and yet, until that time, this man had worked in many films and had done a great deal of stage productions, but not television. Strange is it not?

We have had many interesting visitors from the other side, but because of the label being stuck, the seeking of publicity, we tend not to follow—unless the wish to make contact is expressed. We do keep most of the tapes—for these make very interesting listening—particularly the Christmas ones. We usually, every year, have a special tree just for the Spirit children, and if over the year have received names or told about certain little ones who have departed from this earth—we put little gifts on the tree—streamers, small trumpets—lots of little musical toys. In fact, sometimes it becomes so full that many are put on the floor.

We try to have circle on Christmas Eve, playing carols, and also, once the sitting begins, singing mostly seasonal greetings. To listen to those tapes is quite extraordinary. Hearing the little voices—the stripping of the tree—the tiny instruments blowing away merrily—it's simply beautiful and takes one into Christmas feeling a great love for Christ himself.

Up until now I have not spoken of my religious views. I believe it to be a very personal thing, but I have experienced, just for a few months, intense pain, leading to a major operation. This, in itself, must above all give those who care to read it—some understanding into the power of healing. This goes back to a fall I had about fifteen years ago. I came tumbling off a ladder on to my spine. After a few days of pain my husband was able to help me back on to my feet again, and apart from now and then having some pain, after healing would be perfectly all right, and so enjoyed good health—having always worked and not very often away through sickness until this year.

Yet strangely enough I had decided to give up work and concentrate full-time spiritually. I found that I was having constant pain—more in my legs than my back. I could not stand straight. Although I knew the pain was beginning to show—I hid as much as possible from my husband—for now, even his healing, was not getting through. Let me say that I had forgotten all about the fall I had had years earlier. I thought I was suffering from arthritis—and was desperately afraid—knowing that my mother suffers with this complaint—and now has to be taken everywhere in a wheelchair. I tried to conceal as much as I could from everyone, until the day came when my legs gave out completely. My poor Bill was beside himself with worry—and could not understand why the healing was not making contact with me. I, on the other hand, began to feel that I had something very seriously wrong—far worse than an attack of arthritis. Although apart from knowing, as far back as Christmas, that April would mean something to me, I had no inclination that this could be a health problem—on the contrary, I was shown it as to be something to look forward to.

We had already arranged to spend Easter with my sister and her husband at our dear little caravan which we have based at the coast. My doctor was not happy about my condition and arranged for a leading bone consultant to visit me at my home. I was, of course, after consultation—admitted into our local hospital, and after many tests—it was found that I had indeed very serious injuries to my back—it being fractured. The operation was then arranged for late April on a Thursday morning.

The night before I felt that my life, although still comparatively young, was coming to an end. Strangely I did not feel afraid. I wrote a long letter to my dear husband—light-hearted and yet, between the lines, preparing him. I gave him the letter as he was leaving that night. I went into some sort of vacuum—deep within—peaceful, unafraid. I slept very well that night—in the morning I prepared myself—the intense feeling around me was so peaceful—and when the nurse gave me the pre-medication—I was already relaxed and quite ready. I do remember leaving the ward and hearing the many well-wishers saying, "Good luck, Sheila," but I was, I know, outside of my body—it was most beautiful. I could see the surgeon looking at me above his mask—I wanted to speak to him, but no words would come. I then went into a deep sleep.

I could not believe that I was actually alive. I could hear the familiar voice of my friendly nurse saying, "It's only me, Sheila, just giving you some oxygen," and some time later feeling Bill's hand in mine—looking up with concern at the nurse who was adjusting the transfusion. He looked so ill—I remember thinking. I then spoke to him—and his look of relief was a picture to see. Even with my groggy mind—I shall never forget his face. I could feel the familiar tingling through his hands—filling my body like an electric shock. I squeezed him, letting him know that I was aware—even though I was unable at the time to make conversation.

It took two days before I was able to take stock of my surroundings. My mind was not able to concentrate. I enjoyed the freedom of the world I had been in—and couldn't seem to adjust. My physical strength returned, much to the amazement of the hospital staff. Within three days I walked with a frame—and after just one week was able to walk without any support. The doctors were very impressed by my rapid progress.

I was told, at this time, of the very unusual damage I had inflicted to my spine and they asked my permission for the case to be taken to conference—to which I readily agreed. But it was the following words that stick out in my mind, "How you have managed so long being in such a condition, is in itself, a miracle. Had you continued for very much longer your age would have been against you having such an intricate operation, your body could not have taken it."

After a very short time I returned home—having been away just six weeks in all. I was advised to lay flat most of the time. Bill raised our settee on large wooden blocks—making it easy for me to be able to get on and off. I also had to wear a special corset—which I still do—giving my back support and allowing the bone-graft to knit together. I still cannot sit on an easy chair at the moment, but having a very nice wooden rocking chair, this serves the purpose—and I have found the hours I have sat writing this book—the chair, for me, has become invaluable.

In the very early days, after coming home, I could not express my feelings—not even to Bill, whom I have always been able to talk to—no matter what the problem may be. I did not, in any way, feel that I had been let down by Spirit, and yet I could not link with them at all. I did not even want to talk about it. Whenever Bill or my friends spoke, and the subject invariably would turn to Spirit, I didn't want to know. I was frightened by this—but felt a little easier when my daughter explained that after being under anaesthetic for so long it sometimes took a month, or even longer, before it left the system—and therefore it was quite natural for me to be this way. Bill took me away to convalesce. I felt so sorry for him—he tried to be patient with me, but I still felt strangely different. Everything seemed to be standing out three-dimensionally. My close friends, and those I loved around me, seemed to be showing me their other selves—the part that we hide from others. It was quite horrible. I've always been able to see into people after making contact, but this was very different. As people came into my view they might just as well have stuck two small horns on their foreheads. There they were, asking anxiously after my health, and I seeing the other part of them. I do believe my own spirit was still away from my body—leaving me in some sort of limbo.

My husband was nearly at the end of his tether—having already been through the ordeal of my operation—was now having to suffer this very strange—so very different—woman, whom he thought he knew so well. But suddenly I came back to reality. I could now see my friends as I had always known them—I could now talk again about spirit. I felt very much stronger, not only physically—I was wanting now to catch up with all the spiritual news that I had missed all those weeks. I could not resume circle, and probably will not be able to until early next year, but I have got back to private sittings, finding my clairvoyance even stronger than ever before, and other workers who come to the house—for Bill needs help—having some nights the house overflowing with people—sometimes it is not unusual to find patients in the kitchen—through the dining-room—all the way up the stairs—and I enjoy to be with them—relaxing the newcomers, who are sometimes very frightened, but have come to our door having been told that nothing more can be done for them.

Unfortunately, not everyone receives instant cures from their visits—we do not, and have never, professed to be playing at being God—but we do care, and no one can be more dedicated to his work than Bill—not just because I am prejudiced—or that he happens to be my husband—healing to him is his love and it shows by his sheer devotion behind the scenes. He works, helping so many along the way. I could speak of miracles, but like the circle, it is something that should be treated with the geatest respect. Our door has, and always will be, open for those that wish to seek.

Looking back over my spiritual quest for knowledge—it would take thousands of words—for each day holds many a story. From the beginning, so many years ago, and yet it seems only yesterday when we visited our first medium—we, at that moment, stepped into a world of many wonders. I found, for me, a comforting thought that life does continue on. I still do not know the answers to all the many questions, but shall continue to investigate, and I am ready to accept any logical argument of its non-existence. I would not wish to convert anyone into my belief—it's something that has to be found—and agree that like any religion it holds many loopholes to be criticized, but all along, throughout our searching, disregarding that which we know to be untrue, and we have met, like any other movement, the many weaknesses and charlatans—and yet, after sifting carefully—believe, without any doubt, that there is another world. I am very much aware of this—I've been there and found it to be beautiful.

Having so much time now—something which is indeed a luxury—it gives me an opportunity in taking a good look back, for I have been able to spend many hours on reflection. We have travelled many miles in our search for the truth—from our first meeting—the introduction taking us further and further, step by step, into a spiritual world. Had we gained materially—no, although through the process of time—certainly our way of life—having now, because of our hard efforts, gained us a certain status, but what was around us, our simple, yet lovely home—was due to our own hard work having up until a year ago worked regularly—bringing our financial income comfortably to being without worry.

I'm sure that those who come into contact with us are not aware of the terribly hard struggle that we had in the early years. They see before them two people to be envied—because we appear, on the surface, that we have known no other life and possibly this could be the reason of my frankness—holding to the reader nothing back. I'm not ashamed—I'm proud we made it together. It was a hard struggle—many times we were prepared to give Spirit up—simply because our lack of understanding when things went wrong—the blame was always their fault—never our own, and yet we have so much to thank them for.

I cannot imagine life without Spirit. I try, but I do not feel honestly that Bill and I could have made it on our own. I know plenty of people do, but have they what we have—a love between us and understanding far greater than the average couple—for we have found something other than the material things around. We can talk together for hours upon hours—never being bored with each other. Spirit gave us this gift and we have never grown tired of its wonder—I look back at the all so many unfortunate sick people who have entered this house—each one very special to us—we in no way profess to be God, but we do care and help where we can. I think of dear Frank, our blind friend, who came to us two years ago. On entering he stated to me that he did not believe—and he was only here under protest—he was a very disagreeable man and therefore one could not say that he in anyway was going to be gullible in thinking he might possibly have the chance of regaining his sight, but he was a sticker—and was at least prepared to give us a chance and came every week. Apart from feeling in himself very much better, there was no improvement to his sight—and for eighteen months he patiently came to us—and then he suddenly began to notice changes and found that shapes around him were becoming a lot clearer—then he found that he could see the numbers on car plates.

His wife told us of the night when he had dropped a small tablet—and he said, "You know, I can see that, it's under the chair." "Well," she said, "If you can see it so well, you jolly well pick it up,"—which he did. Since then much progress had taken place—he now comes without his white stick—he can read. Yes, he can see. This was not an overnight miracle—two years it has taken, but what's two years in a blind man's life when you hear him say, "I see the leaves changing to their autumn colours. I can see the birds."

One might say, "Why, if Spirit is so powerful, did it take so long." I cannot answer—maybe it is to teach us patience—and if we, the workers, are prepared to accept—why not the patient. My husband will not—even though Frank has improved—give up the healing on him. One day soon this man's sight will be completely recovered—then, and only then, will Bill say, "You are healed." It would be only right to say that over the two years Frank's views have changed somewhat. He now enjoys his life to the full—his understanding of Spirit is very much changed. I'm sure, given the chance, he could be quite boring with his attitude now towards spiritual healing—telling anyone who may be in his contact—of this amazing gift—and forgetting how he was just a little while ago very much against—and very embarrassed should it be mentioned that he, himself, had visited a healer.

A few weeks ago we were approached by our local spiritualist church to take a service for them—which we agreed to do—although apart from the odd one or two—do not want to become involved—as we were taking regular services in the past—having over a number of years served probably hundreds. We did decide—partly thinking it would be nice for many of our friends who visit our house—might like—being so local—to experience the service in a spiritualist church, for they had, apart from knowing us, no knowledge of the religion. They were enthusiastic and on the Sunday of the service, as we entered on to the rostrum—I was pleased to see so many familiar faces—and noticed that sitting amongst them were quite a few young people whom I had not met before, but was aware of their obvious connections with our friends.

It was a good feeling—being inside the church—a lovely building. I had not been inside it before—although in the preceeding years we had served Cheshunt Church, but at that time the meetings were held in the local labour hall. Now they had moved into the college—which contains many different buildings within its walls—for the college was used as a civic centre—therefore many functions take place—and this beautiful chapel serves for many purposes in the borough.

I looked quickly across at Bill, who was sitting the other side of the chairman, but did not catch his attention. I could see at a glance that he was already making contact with his Spirit helpers—I turned my attention to the chairman who was just about to start the service. He seemed strangely familiar to me—and yet I couldn't quite place him. I heard him, as was usual, welcoming us both—then was surprised to hear him say, "Mrs. Macey probably does not remember, but she is responsible for my being here. I visited her home many years ago—a complete sceptic. She said many things which, at the time, meant nothing, but over a time her words became uncannily true, and as one can see, my views are now very much changed."

He smiled at me—many years ago I thought how long I wonder—so many people. This made me reflect back—remembering the many sittings I would give to the seeker—the funniest being a young man who came into my little room—very nervous—"Don't be afraid," I remember saying to him, "You will find me quite natural, nothing will suddenly appear to cause you fright. Spirit is not at all, as you may at first imagine." How I recall so vividly, him sitting on the small armchair opposite me. "I'll just close my eyes that's all—you just sit back, relax and enjoy the sitting."

I began, but after a few moments I could hear movement—then a shout of "Good God." I could not resist the temptation to look—and there, perched happily on this poor man's shoulder, was our old tabby cat that had somehow got on to the window ledge and had been hidden by the closed curtains. My sense of humour immediately took stock of the situation—and I laughingly said, "Was he all right," chastising our cat at the same time. All he said was, "Thank God I've got a good strong heart, otherwise you may have had a corpse on your hands." I'm happy to say that we still keep contact with this man after all those years—and he loves to tell people about—as he puts it—his narrow escape from death.

The music started, I brought myself back quickly as the congregation began to sing the opening hymn. Memories, beautiful memories—how fortunate I am to have seen so many—sometimes almost unbelievable happenings—and yet I am an ordinary individual—nothing special about me—or Bill come to that. Yet through this remarkable power—I have been privileged in having this wonderful gift. I wonder why God chose me—for I do realize he is my power—and my love for him and Christ has grown closer—as the years go steadily by.

The music stopped—and I listened intensely as my husband

began his address. I enjoyed to sit back—and link closely with him—giving as much support—knowing full well that he, in turn, will do the same for me when I take the stand. I was not surprised to hear him speak about healing although the subject varied considerably—depending on who would be controlling him. This night it was evident our friend, the spirit doctor, was giving his inspirations—and as Bill's voice spoke—I could see him clairvoyantly—and as was always, fascinated, for the doctor was a very different build to my husband and overshadowing him as it was—it looked quite extraordinary.

Yes, it felt good to be back upon a platform—although I would not wish to work in this way—only on an occasion. I'll invite our friends back for coffee, I decided, as Bill sat down—and once again we prepared for the next hymn. I'll ask them as soon as the service is over—and after that thought—my demonstration was now ready—and I stood up, feeling at that moment so uplifted. It felt like sailing on air—I wondered why I should feel so very light-headed. I happily made contact from one to another—enjoying this feeling immensely, the congregation sensing my obvious excitement, joined in—making a truly lovely atmosphere.

All too soon the chairman called us to a halt—it's over—time had, as was usual, overtaken us—and we all sang the last hymn. I know why I felt this way—it all suddenly made sense. There I was—in a church—linking with God—taking a service, the first since my operation. It felt just as if I had come home. How appropriate that we should be singing together—*Nearer My God to Thee*. I knew I was. I wonder how many out there were—I thought as we closed the service in prayer.

To my pleasure all our friends accepted our invitation to come home with us—and we also invited the young people—who seemed enthralled and genuinely thrilled at the invitation. On arriving home, within minutes, the house was filled with happy conversation—and the refreshments were quickly seen to—and then we sat back and waited for the avalanche of questions—each eager to speak—sometimes interrupting one another with their enthusiasm.

One young couple, in particular, held my attention. I watched them as they sat next to one another on our settee. The young man was asking my husband how long he had been involved spiritually.

Bill looked across at me, "Would it be about twenty years? he said, I nodded. "What gave you the inclination to investigate?" asked the young man. "Well it's a long story," said Bill. The pretty young girl by his side looked carefully at the both of us, "Why, you must have been young," she said. "About your age, I should think," I answered. "Was you frightened by it all?" came the question. "Petrified," I replied. "Did you meet someone like yourselves in the beginning that made you interested, or did it just happen." I smiled at this interesting couple—so young—so inexperienced. Answering the young man, I carefully said, "Do you realize having you here this night has turned back the clock—you could so easily be Bill and I, we have just completed a full circle, ending up this night where we began, as all good stories should, at the beginning. Only now you are the seekers, thirsting for knowledge, so if you are prepared to listen to this story then I shall begin . . ."

* * *

I could not complete my story, without first including the many funny, sometimes hilarious situations that I have faced throughout my adventures within the spiritualist movement. To appreciate the fun I experienced, I have recorded them in story fashion. Relive with me, as I take you behind the scenes . . .

THE DRAGON'S CURE

"Hi, Jill," I said to the patient, as I entered the small ward in which I worked. "Sorry," I whispered, putting my hand to my lips, as I observed that she was talking on the trolley pay-phone which was available to the patients. Jill acknowledged me with a quick nod of her head, "Hang on," she said, as I was about to make my exit, "Somebody wants to speak to you on the telephone." "Who me," I replied, in shocked surprise.

As I had known Jill only a few days I couldn't imagine who could possibly want to speak to me personally. "Yes, hurry up," she said, holding her hand over the mouthpiece. "Who is it," I whispered. Jill smiled at me—it was so lovely to see her smile—as for the little time I had helped nurse her she had been very ill. Yet somehow, I had managed to get through to her the power of healing, and her response was almost miraculous.

She pushed the receiver into my hand and I nervously said, "Hello." A clear-cut well-educated voice reached my ear, "Sheila, may I call you by your christian name? This is Claire. Jill has been telling me all about you—I would dearly love to meet you and your husband and talk over with you both your knowledge of the spiritual world." "Why, certainly," I replied. It was always pleasing to be able to talk to those interested enough to listen. I think it was because of our very down-to-earth approach to the subject that we never seemed to lack friends.

"Are you free on Sunday?" Claire asked. "I believe so," I said, desperately trying to remember what arrangements, if any, had been made for the coming week-end. "Well, how about coming for tea. I'll expect you about four o'clock," although the voice sounded charming, I detected from it someone who was used to being obeyed, "Jill will give you my address." "Fine, I'll see you then," I said, still a little bewildered by the rather hasty way my Sunday had been arranged.

I passed the receiver back to an eager outstretched hand, and overheard the following conversation, "Yes, she sounds extremely nice." I smiled, and walked over to the bed, and although it had already been made by the early shift, I automatically began to tidy the pillows. The last exchange of goodbyes were made and the bell rang as the receiver was replaced.

"Whoever was that?" I said to Jill who was sitting on the freshly-made hospital bed. "The matron of a lovely hospital in Highgate," said my patient. "You've got to be kidding. Matrons don't go about inviting lowly auxiliary nurses to take tea with them." "I'm not kidding," said Jill, "She happens to be a very dear friend of mine and I have been telling her all about you both."

As Jill chatted on my mind couldn't seem to take in what was happening to me—for in those days, the early sixties, hospital life had not changed from their very old-fashioned attitude to the staff. The word "Matron" was as good as the word "God" and one practically shivered at the very mention of such a being, and here was I, a mere auxiliary, not even a qualified nurse, going to take tea with her.

"Sheila, wake up, I'm talking to you." "Oh, sorry," I replied, still in a state of shock. I pulled myself together. "You'll like her, she's not a bit like you think," Jill carried on, trying, I'm sure, to make me feel a little easier. "You mustn't be scared of her, you'll find her quite human." "I hope you are right," I retorted.

"Oh gosh," I exclaimed, "I've just remembered Keith's coming to us on Sunday for tea. I can't put him off." Dear Keith, he was a great friend to us both and he had had a rough time of it and was now just beginning to settle after the trauma of a broken marriage. "What shall I do," I looked at Jill miserably. "Cheer up, take Keith with you, Claire won't mind. I'll give her a ring and explain." "Well, if you're sure," I said, with a little doubt in my mind.

I received a nod from my patient and hurried back to the main ward and was greeted by some very disgruntled staff. "Come along now, nurse, you must not spend so much time with Nurse Fielding. I know she has been very ill, but she really must not keep you chatting so long. There's six bed-baths to be done before doctor's round, so get cracking before sister catches you."

I obediently turned tail to the sluice and quickly loaded the trolley with two enamel jugs of hot water. I piled the bowls on top of one another and rattled noisily along the corridor, having great difficulty trying not to spill any of the water from the over-filled jugs. I backed my way through the folding doors of the ward and made my way to the first patient on my list. Mrs. Sparrow, bed four, I confirmed. "Here we are," I said to the poor little soul that was looking at me with large frightened eyes. She had only been admitted the previous night and was very, very scared. I smiled warmly at her. "I'm going to give you a lovely wash, you'll feel so much better," I assured her, and so my day's work went quickly by and I had no more time to worry about the earlier happenings of the day. In fact, I had been home some time before the penny dropped.

It was during dinner that evening that the words came rushing out—"And she's asked us to have tea with her on Sunday." "So," said Bill. "Well, don't you think it's extraordinary," I remarked, "After all she is a matron!" I emphasised the word "Matron," excitedly. "I can't see anything special about it," said my husband, he was never impressed by social standings, "But I'll grant you it's unusual for one so high in the medical profession to be interested in our spiritual work. What about Keith? You did invite him over on Sunday, you know." "Oh, it's O.K., at least I think so. Jill said she would explain and that it will probably be alright to take Keith with us. Anyway, she will confirm tomorrow. I expect she is interested in healing," I said. "We did have marvellous results with that nurse," replied Bill. "You mean Jill," I said. "Yes," said Bill, "Mind you she did respond quickly to you which made things easier."

We were very excited with the results we were getting in healing. Keith, my husband, and I, were experimenting into the power that one could eject from concentration of the mind, and Jill had been one to experience that power. But we were in the very early stages of investigation. We had, however, experienced many weird and wonderful things and the possible opportunity of demonstrating this amazing gift to someone within the medical profession was indeed a bonus. I looked forward to the approaching Sunday, yet I couldn't control my nervousness, and when Sunday finally arrived I was decidedly edgy and a little short-tempered. "Calm down," said Bill, "She won't bite."

I busied myself around the house until Keith arrived. "What's all this about then," I heard him saying to my husband, as they came in from the hall. "Hi, Keith," I said, "Got you best bib and tucker on? Tea and cucumber sandwiches for you, my man," I said laughingly. "I hope not," said Bill, "Cucumber repeats something awful." "Perhaps it will be cress and paste," I said. "No," said Keith, joining in the fun, "It will be bread and dripping." "Smashing," said I, licking my lips, "Well, are we nearly ready?" "I think so," said Bill.

I looked approvingly at my husband who was very smart in his best suit, worn under protest I might add, as I thought it wouldn't look to good to be in casuals, which is how he preferred to dress. But today he had given in to my constant persuasion. The three of us left the house laughing and joking, still listing things that might be on the menu.

The journey took about an hour during which time we happily chattered together, until the hospital came in view, and suddenly, all went quiet. The driveway was clearly marked with a sign saying "Matron" and we slowly drove along it. It twisted and turned for some little way and then as Keith turned the car out of a sharp bend a beautiful bungalow appeared on the scene and standing at the door was a young woman dressed in the uniform of a matron. On seeing us arrive she smiled and walked towards the car.

I could feel my heart miss a beat. "Gosh, I'm scared," I whispered, but before anybody could answer me she was opening the car door. We exchanged greetings and I introduced Bill and Keith. "Excuse the uniform," she said, as she guided us towards the bungalow, "Only I have my rounds at 5.30 p.m. "Oh, that's O.K.," said Keith casually, "It's quite an experience to be socializing with a real live matron." I could have killed him for that remark, but if she was annoyed, she didn't show it. "Do come in and meet Mother". With a gesture of her hand she moved us towards the doorway.

We were escorted into a rather elegant room. It was very clinical, as I had imagined, white walls and doors, which was broken by a small painting of a landscape. The room contained a small settee, which was of cottage style, and had loose covers neatly fitted to it. There was a nest of small tables stacked tidily in one corner—these were made out of dark oak. On the long white window-sill stood some photographs in gold frames.

"Mother," our hostess called, "Our friends have arrived." "You must also meet Jasper," she said, "He is in the garden." With that she left the room leaving us standing uncertainly, but only for a moment. Before we had a chance to make any remark the door opened and standing within its framework, looking not too appraisingly at the three of us, stood a large lady with a false smile on her face. She greeted us—hand outstretched. "You must be Sheila," she said, as I gave her my hand, "Claire has told me about the remarkable story of the miracle cure of Nurse Fielding. Of course, my daughter is inclined to over-dramatize. I, personally, cannot believe such a story."

Her stinging words hurt, but I took a deep breath, expecting any second that Bill or Keith would retaliate. I had visions of us all turning tail as fast as we could back down the pathway whence we had come. However, Jasper saved the day! The ice-cold embarrassing silence of the room changed as an over excited bundle of white fur came bounding in. The little poodle was absolutely thrilled to see us. "Hello there," I said, and patted its furry body enthusiastically. I loved animals and Jasper knew this for he was jumping madly up at me. "That's enough," laughed Claire, as I was nearly knocked backwards by the force of the small but very compact little body.

"Do sit down all of you," our hostess said, retrieving Jasper by his gold-studded collar, "He'll settle in a moment." The men remained standing whilst Mother and I sat down—then, like gentlemen, having first gestured to Claire to be seated, sat themselves down. Claire was still holding Jasper by his collar, who was not at all happy with the situation as he wanted to investigate these interesting visitors who had invaded his home. I took stock of the tall, slim girl before us. She was in her mid-thirties. She was especially young to be a matron. She was attractive, and yet not pretty, with nice eyes that seemed to light up when speaking to you. I liked her, but I wasn't so sure about her mother, who showed that she definitely did not approve of her daughter's visitors. She was not above showing her disapproval by childishly sulking. She sat in her chair, ignoring us all, pretending to be pre-occupied with one of her finger-nails.

"I'll bring the trolley in and we'll have some tea," said our hostess. "Mother, entertain our visitors will you." said Claire, as she left the room, not waiting for an answer. It seemed an uncomfortable length of time before she returned. I broke the stony silence. "Jasper's a lovely poodle," I remarked. The little dog was barking excitedly, telling his mistress, no doubt, that he wished to be allowed in the room where her visitors were, especially as he had picked up the scent of my own little corgi. Mother answered me without looking up, still intent on being decidedly awkward. "Yes, he is," and promptly remained silent once again.

Bill spoke about the grounds and the beautiful outlook from the bungalow. Keith and I also made idle chatter, agreeing that the grounds were indeed quite delightful. To our relief Claire entered the room. The fine bone china made a gentle clatter as the wheels of the tea-trolley made contact with the deep pile carpet. I couldn't resist taking a peep at the lower half of the trolley. I smiled to myself on seeing tiny slices of brown and white bread and butter, cut decoratively into triangular shapes. A two-tiered cake-stand stood next to the sandwiches. This held a home-made fruit cake on the bottom stand and tiny iced fancy cakes on the top.

"We'll have tea first and then you must tell me all about the results you have been getting with healing," said Claire, "I am so interested—and perhaps you could give Mother some, she's not been at all well recently, have you Mother?" Claire was looking at her sympathetically. I shivered at the prospect, expecting at any moment to be told, in no uncertain terms, from this formidable lady, just what she thought of us. Mother had no time to express her opinion as there was quite a commotion going on in the hall. "Oh good," our hostess said, "That must be Teddy."

As she spoke in came an enormous man—weighing all of twenty stone of muscle and flesh. "My brother, Teddy," said Claire proudly. He took my hand, which quickly disappeared from view inside his own, and with a great smile, greeted me warmly. I could feel my whole body tremble with his great strength. He then exchanged greetings with the men. "I'm so pleased I was able to make it," he said, "I got held up and didn't think I would be able to get away." As he was speaking his great body moved towards his mother, who smiled sweetly at him. He plonked a smacking kiss on her cheek. "How have you been—any better since my last visit?"

Claire spoke before her mother could answer, "No, Teddy, she's not been at all well. I'm quite worried about her. I was just saying before you arrived that maybe Bill and Keith could help. You remember the story I told you about Jill." I watched his face intently as he looked affectionately at his sister. "Why not give it a try," he asked his mother, as he looked round at the three of us. "I can't say that I understand what you do, but if you can help my mother, I would be much obliged—she's caused us a few problems just lately." Smiling warmly, he took hold of his mother's hand, "Haven't you darling?" She nodded, and wiped her eyes with a delicate lace handkerchief.

During this time I had already used my mediastic powers and linked within this lady. Her health was indeed causing some concern, but I'm afraid a large part of the problem was mental. This lady had been thoroughly spoilt by her two children since the death of their father, and had enjoyed a pampered life, and this she was not prepared to give up in any way. Poor Claire, I thought, she may be the boss of the hospital, but in the home, mother ruled.

With all her nursing experience she could not see this because of her devotion for her mother. The men readily agreed to give mother some healing.

We had passed a pleasant hour, enjoying the refreshments which had been so nicely prepared. Claire left for a short time to do her rounds, leaving us in the hands of her brother Teddy, who was very good company. I now felt quite at home and Bill and Keith also seemed to be more relaxed. The room was filled with the deep voices of the men's eager chatter. I tried very hard to make conversation with mother, but found it to be a very trying experience. I gave up the attempt and turned my attention to the men's conversation.

Claire returned from her duties, but looked so different. She had changed from her uniform and now wore a neat grey woollen dress which appeared to make her look much taller than she really was. "I see you are all getting on nicely. I could hear you as I walked up the garden path," she said happily, "Well now, are we to witness this healing power of yours? I really am very interested." I could believe her for she was so full of enthusiasm.

"Right," said Keith, looking at Bill apprehensively. My husband slowly stood up. "May we wash our hands," he said. Teddy showed them the way whilst I asked Claire if we could use an upright chair for mother to sit on. Immediately a chair was produced and Claire's mother, most reluctantly, was helped on to it. We waited for the men to return. I knew they were nervous. The room was suddenly devoid of noise and the silence was unnerving. I whispered a word of encouragement to Bill, as he and Keith returned. I then joined Claire who was sitting on the sofa. Teddy had already made himself comfortable, legs outstretched, waiting inquisitively for the forthcoming proceedings to start. Mother, with a look of complete distaste on her face at the whole affair, sat very upright and alert on the chair.

"Just relax," said Keith, as in unison both men laid their hands on her greying head. She never moved a muscle—just stared straight into space—whilst the men continued to work steadily on her. After a short time, mother suddenly slumped forward in what appeared to be a deep sleep. I knew from past experience that she was unconscious. "Isn't it marvellous," Claire whispered to me. I wasn't so sure—I didn't like the look of mother at all. Bill looked down at her, and saw with an anxious glance at Keith, that he was showing signs of distinct panic.

Unaware of the drama, our friend, the matron, was by now overwhelmed. She nudged me excitedly. "Look, mother's gone." You're not kidding, I thought, she's gone all right. I could see the men struggling to get her back. Oh God, I had visions of a corpse on our hands and that great hulk of a man making mincemeat of us all. "What power—it's incredible." Claire's voice was now raised with the excitement of it all. Her brother made no comment, but was looking on in amazement. I saw mother's body slowly lean towards Bill and he promptly pushed her back on to the chair.

By now many minutes had passed and still no sign of life was coming from their patient. Keith looked over at me. I knew he was desperate, but then so was I. In fact, I was beginning to feel physically sick, and by the look of Bill, he felt likewise. Every bit of blood had drained from his face, making him look most peculiar. Once again Claire nudged me and whispered, "It takes an awful lot out of them both. I can see that mother will be so grateful." I nearly choked on my own spittle on hearing that last remark, for I was now lost for words, and could only nod in reply. Never had we experienced anything like this. We had used our powers and knew that it was possible to put a patient into a semi-conscious state, but had never really seen it happen—and from where I was sitting this lady looked to be in more than a state of semi-consciousness—more like a deep coma, and it didn't look as if she was ever coming back.

Mother would indeed be grateful. I grimaced at the thought of being haunted by her for the rest of our lives, when suddenly it happened. Yes, oh yes, I saw her move, slowly, ever so slowly, but she was coming to. The look of relief on my husband's face was a picture. Keith, had left the room. I knew where he had gone—fright had had its effect on him that's for sure. Teddy lifted his great frame from the chair and went to his mother's aid. She was still sitting on the chair in her rigid upright position. Whatever had happened to her certainly showed. Her expression looked exactly like the cartoon character of Tom in "Tom and Jerry"—when he had his head beaten in and the birdies were tweet, tweet, tweeting around him.

Whether it was relief or tension, or my nerves had suddenly got the better of me, I don't know, but the upmost difficulty in quelling the laughter that kept rising in me. I managed to keep my composure for the rest of the evening, but before we had left the driveway, whilst still waving our good-byes, I began to laugh, for never had I seen such a complete change in anybody as I had this night. The funny thing was that her sweet smile and dazed expression didn't match her face—she looked much better as a dragon. We drove home, tears of laughter running down our faces. Our brush with the matron's mother was an experience that we were not ever likely to forget.

STRIKE A LIGHT

I yawned loudly, as I came down the stairs, still groggy with sleep. The postman had woken me with a noisy rat-tat on the door. Some people say they enjoy the postman's knock, but I had gone to bed very late the night before and was suffering from the after-effects of an extremely nice birthday party given by one of our close friends—and didn't feel in the least bit enthusiastic about being woken so suddenly.

My head felt heavy as I bent to pick up the small pile of letters from the doormat. I walked unsteadily into the kitchen, throwing the offending mail on to the dinette table. As far as I was concerned the most important thing of the day was to find the alka seltzer; good, they were close at hand. I popped a couple of tablets into a glass of water and watched as they slowly fizzed up and disappeared, leaving tiny globlets of bubbles rushing up and down the glass. I swallowed the lot in one big gulp and burped noisily. Now for some coffee—then perhaps I would feel a little more human.

I waited patiently for the kettle to boil, my mind going over the previous night's jolly get-together. It was fun, I mused, although I had acted a bit of a fool pretending to be an opera singer. I couldn't help smiling when I remembered the antics we had got up to as we acted out an awful crescendo of *Madame Butterfly*.

I made the coffee and was feeling much better as I turned my attention to the envelopes on the table—three brown ones—must be bills, I thought, as I tossed them aside, and one white, I looked closely at the white envelope—not recognising the neat handwriting. I quickly slipped a knife into the corner and slit it cleanly open. "The Women's Institute" was the paper's letter-heading. "Dear Mrs. Macey," I read, "I wonder if you would be kind enough to give our group a talk on clairvoyancy"—I smiled at that, but continued reading, "As I have been requested by our ladies to contact you and hopefully persuade you to come to our club and demonstrate. We would, of course, do our best to co-operate regarding any equipment you may need, but must stress that we do hire the local school and therefore lighting may be a problem. However I am sure we will do our best if you would consider coming along. We meet on a Tuesday evening and the following dates, underlined, are vacant. Please find enclosed a stamped addressed envelope, and we await, in anticipation, a favourable reply. Yours sincerely, Mrs. Bragget."

I digested the letter carefully, reading over and over again the extraordinary point about lighting. "What a laugh," I said to Bill, as I presented him with the letter. It was almost lunch-time before Bill finally decided he would greet the day. He held the letter in one hand whilst scratching his untidy uncombed head with the other. He looked, for all the world, as though he had had many late nights and too much drink for some time past instead of one night's small celebration, as he stood there with great bags under his eyes.

Bill smiled, as I had done, as he read the contents of the letter. "Are you going," said Bill. "No, but we are," I emphasised the word "We". "Oh no," said my husband, as he shook his untidy head, "I'm not going to talk to a hall full of giggling ladies—it will be murder. I mean, you've only got to read this letter to see what they expect from us. I ask you, clairvoyancy—special equipment, what do they think we are, some sort of magic weirdos." My husband, having said his piece, drank his coffee—still holding the letter in his hand.

A mischievous smile came over his face and then he let out a quiet laugh. "We could have them on"—he licked his lips excitedly at the prospect. "Oh, go on with you," I laughed, knowing full well he was joking, but found the thought very tempting. After some gentle persuasion my husband agreed to accompany me and so I arranged the date, making it quite clear that we required nothing out of the ordinary for the proposed talk and demonstration.

The appointed Tuesday evening arrived. That particular day had been one of those days. I had been held up due to a rail strike. There had been only one or two trains getting through, but somehow I managed to force myself on to one. That was bad enough, but having done so, I found myself in a carriage designed to take approximately fifteen commuters but holding at least forty bedraggled occupants; as to add to our other miseries it was pouring of rain. Those who were lucky enough to have found a seat were punished by having wet brollies dripping down their necks placed on the luggage rail by their travelling companions. Yes, I thought, you could always guarantee it would rain when the unions decided to go slow. I stood rigidly between two other unfortunates, who, like me, were unable to move a muscle.

I passed this uncomfortable time, however, by watching huge raindrops running down from a large black umbrella and forming a little stream of water which, as the train rumbled along the unsteady track, eventually fell with great blobs on to the rim of the gentleman's hat who was sitting directly underneath.

Another distraction to take our minds away from our uncomfortable journey was a lady who stood quite near me who dropped her shopping bag—how she managed this in the crush I do not know—but for the next few minutes we were all trying to retrieve the brussels sprouts and tomatoes which had escaped. If that wasn't bad enough, the wet fish she had bought for her cat, for which she kept apologising, had also fallen out of the bag. No wonder there had been a fishy smell in the over full compartment. The expression "packed like sardines" was certainly now a reality. Once the offending articles had been returned to their owner, I again turned my attention to the dripping brolly. By this time the drips had gathered in the rim and were spilling over and running down the back of the gentleman's coat collar. He seemed, however, to be completely unaware of what was happening to him.

At last we pulled into my station and I pushed myself forwards. I practically fell out backwards when I reached the door. I hurriedly made my way out of the station, feeling wet, cold and miserable. As I reached the road where I lived, the street lights suddenly went out, which made the last part of my journey equally frustrating. It was mid-November and therefore very dark as the lights from the houses were also extinguished as the power supply was cut.

"Would you believe it—now there's a power strike," said a lady, who was walking behind me. I don't know what the world is coming to," she retorted, "They reckon we are going to have these power cuts at least until Christmas." She passed before I had a chance to reply.

I was grateful at that moment to see the headlights of a car, shining like a beacon, showing me that I had nearly reached my house. I fumbled for the door key trying desperately to hold on to my umbrella that was being buffeted about in the strong wind and rain. I entered the house, thankful to be home. Shaking myself and shivering with the cold, I made my way into the kitchen. "Second shelf up," I said out loud, as I reached for the candles which I had bought the previous week for such an emergency. I said a small prayer as my hand touched the smooth wax, pleased that I had found them so quickly. I had also placed a box of matches nearby and as the wick slowly burned it gave off a small light.

Bill arrived home a few moments later, and I was pleased, for I knew he had a battery lantern in the car which would help as I prepared a meal. We were lucky, however, as the lights were suddenly restored, making my chores a little easier, especially as we were in such a hurry to eat and attend our promised talk. "You're late," said my husband, giving me his usual kiss on the cheek greeting. "Go slow on the trains," I answered, "I had a terrible journey home." "We'll have to make do tonight," I said, taking some bacon out of the fridge. I pulled off four rashers and placed them on the grill—checked that I had sufficient eggs—and proceeded to butter the bread. "I'll nip upstairs and get shaved, it will save time," said Bill. "O.K. dear," I answered him. "There's a clean shirt on a coat-hanger on the bedroom door," I shouted at him as he ran up the stairs.

I finished buttering the bread and quickly began to open a can of beans. Calamity, I caught my fingers on the jagged edge of the tin. Blood from my fingers began to drip all over the work surface. "Damn," I said out loud, as I ran my fingers under the tap, feeling the soreness of the cut. "Where's my clean vest and pants?" shouted Bill from upstairs. I could have screamed with vexation, but took a controlled deep breath and called out, "Top drawer of the dresser, dear." "Right," came back the lighthearted reply.

I remembered I had put a tin of plaster strips in the sideboard drawer in the lounge and quickly attended to my cuts. I suddenly became aware of something burning—Oh God, the bacon, I thought, as I flew back into the kitchen. "Something down there is burning," said my husband's voice. It was burnt all right. Ugly black smoke was escaping from the grill. "Damn, damn, damn," I said, throwing the unrecognisable pieces of bacon into the rubbish bin, "I've only got two rashers left in the fridge, we'll just have to make do."

Our problems seemed to continue until we eventually got into the car. I felt utterly exhausted—the only good thing that had happened so far was the rain stopping. Bill switched on the ignition and we were away. We had a fair way to go so I relaxed—thankful that we were not going to be too late. "Still, they can't start without us, can they kid," said my husband affectionately, "Look's like we might be coming to the school now."

I looked out of the car window and saw a brightly lit building. As we turned into the playground I took note of the many cars that were parked. On finding a convenient parking space, and locking the car, we made our way to the entrance of the school. That was when the noise hit us, high-pitched excited voices making a terrible row. As we followed the sound it got louder and louder. We encountered white-painted swing-doors with frosted glass, in an oval shape, half-way up them. On entering the hall we saw that there was at least three hundred females. I don't think I have ever heard such a racket as they were making, and for a moment felt quite ashamed of my own sex.

Bill looked shattered at the sight of so many women and looked most odd amongst us all being the only male in sight. From the look on his face he was also petrified. So much for all his bravado about women, I thought. One move from the crowd towards him and you wouldn't see him for dust. We stood hesitantly just inside the door. On seeing us, a rather large lady walked towards us. "Mr. and Mrs. Macey," she said, with her hand outstretched in greeting. Taking her hand, I introduced myself and Bill. "Sorry about the noise," she shouted, "Only we've got a full house tonight—word gets around you know. They love it mind you, we are all scared, but when I first mentioned the idea it caused such a great interest—hence the large crowd." All this was being said as we were escorted to the table at the end of the large hall.

As we made our way past the assorted female race—all shapes and sizes, young and old, short and tall, Bill still looked panic stricken. We thankfully sat down on the chairs provided as we reached the table. Bill, with shaking hands, immediately began to roll a cigarette, not daring to raise his eyes. I, on the other hand, took stock of the situation. My ears had now grown quite accustomed to the din. This could turn out to be a really good night, I decided, just gain their attention and we'll be away. They must be keen to have turned up on such a cold night.

I nearly jumped out of my skin as a wooden hammer came crashing down on the table. "Silence please, ladies." A sudden hush descended over the large hall and all eyes turned towards the three of us at the table. "Now let's start tonight's proceedings by welcoming our guests," said the chairlady. "I should also like to thank you all for coming," she said enthusiastically. "And I know that we have all been looking forward eagerly to the talk and demonstration to be given by Mr. and Mrs. Macey." She smiled at us as we were introduced. "I will leave the evening entirely in your hands, but before doing so, as it is our custom, the ladies would like to make you feel most welcome." "Here, here," I heard someone say from the large audience, and this was followed by clapping, which sounded like thunder, as they all applauded in unison. "It's all yours," said our host keenly, as she sat down.

Bill looked nervously at me amid the noise of the clapping. "Ready?" "Yes," I nodded, "You start first." He rose slowly from his chair, and as he did so, the hall became silent once more, each face looking at my husband's apprehensively. He rubbed his hands together giving himself time to gather his thoughts. He began with a quavering voice, "Good evening, ladies, how many of you expected to see some odd-looking people here tonight?" Quite a few put up their hands to the question. "And how many of you are expecting to see Spirit communication," my husband continued. More hands went up hesitantly. "Well, I don't think my wife and I are so very odd, in fact, we look almost human." This caused laughter. "As for seeing Spirit," Bill continued, "I can assure you we are not about to have any unearthly ghostly experience here tonight." Again laughter. Silly giggles could be heard also. "However, ladies, we do hope to be able to enlighten you on the subject."

I looked upon the rows and rows of interested faces—listening to every word that my husband was saying. Apart from the odd titter here and there, Bill had captured his audience, and I could feel that they were being very receptive towards him, but they were also rather frightened—hence the nervous giggle, particularly when the word "ghost" and things that go bump in the night were mentioned.

My husband was trying to dispense the idea that surrounded the Spirit world which, over the past, had been caused by some oddities, that ghostly and peculiar things would happen, when, all of a sudden, without any warning, the lights went out. First an uncanny silence fell, and then for a second, pandemonium, all hell let loose within that hall. I heard chairs being knocked over, amongst screams and cries of "Oh God, he's turned the bloody lights out, and he's nowhere near the switch." "Order, ladies, order please," I shouted, trying to find the hammer in the inky blackness. I couldn't see Bill, or for that matter, the dear lady in the chair, and I don't mind admitting I too was a little scared, not of the total darkness, but of the obvious riot which was about to take off at any second unless something was done.

"They're like witches," I heard a voice near me say, "They can do all sorts of weird things. I'm getting out of here before they materialize one of their spirits." With that remark there were more screams and sounds of shuffling feet. By now my eyes had adjusted to the darkness and I could just make out dozens of shapes moving towards the centre of the hall in order to get out of the door. "Bill, do something," I said, looking towards him in the murky light. No reply. "Bill, do you hear me, do something," I pleaded.

Then, like a miracle, the lights came on again. The scene before me looked like something out of a movie—practically an empty hall with chairs scattered everywhere. There was, however, quite a large crowd milling around the doorway in an endeavour to get out. I turned to look for Bill and was amazed to see the still form of my husband slumped across the table in a dead faint.

Eventually some sort of order was attained and our remaining ladies returned to their seats, and Bill, who made a pretty quick recovery, was able to participate in the rest of the evening's programme—although he did look decidedly peaky.

It wasn't until we arrived home that I learned the truth of my husband's sudden attack of unconsciousness. Apparently, the chairlady, who was sitting immediately next to Bill, and who was still holding the wooden hammer in her hand, on the shock of seeing the lights go out, put her arm out in panic and hit him with such force in the solar plexus that it knocked him senseless. Bill, being the gentleman that he is, left the ladies to draw their own conclusions which were, of course, a completely different story of the night they were entertained at "The Women's Institute".

I WANT TO COME TO YOU, DEAR

"How much longer are you going to be?" I heard Bill, my husband, calling to me, "It's a hell of a way—so get your skates on." "O.K., two more minutes," I shouted back at him. Yes, Sheila, that looks really good, you clever old thing, I complimented myself—trying, with much difficulty, to see the back view, which was quite impossible. Not a bad bit of material, and very cheap. I smiled at my reflection in the mirror. They'll never know it cost only ten shillings.

I sometimes wonder at my brilliance—searching through that old chest outside the curtain shop in the High Road—loads of all sorts, but that pretty blue and white spotted silk had not passed my expert eye. Blooming cheek that old lady had—grabbing hold of it just as I was about to investigate its size. I'm glad she scratched her arm on the piece of wire jutting out of the box—that will teach her, she knew I was going to have it. I then reproached myself for having such evil thoughts. Still, to be honest the colour suits me better than it would her.

My husband's voice, now agitated, hurried me along. So with a quick approving look at myself I ran down the stairs. "How's that then?" I said to Bill, turning round like a model. "Yes, it looks fine—now get your coat on so we can be off." Like a scolded child I silently put my coat over my arm. "It's too warm to wear my coat in the car," I answered Bill, before he spoke—seeing his expression. "Right, here's the A to Z. I've turned up the pages we shall need."

My husband was now patiently standing at the front door, as I said, "Hang on," and ran back into the lounge to take a last look in the long mirror on the wall. Yes, smashing, I thought. "Right-ho, let's go," I said, and out I went, leaving Bill sighing heavily as he shut the door.

I settled comfortably in the car, noticing as I did, a young kiddie busily fixing a piece of rope over the hanging branch of a tree which stood amongst others, in a uniformed row, to separate the allotments from the estate. He'll never make it, not that way, I thought, as my husband started up the engine and pulled away from the kerb. I couldn't resist turning round to watch the youngster until we turned the corner. I must remember to take a look tomorrow on my way to work to see if he managed it, I told myself. It will be too dark by the time we get home tonight.

"Cor! Did you see that," I said to Bill, "Old Mrs. Moffet's got company." I turned my head in order to be nosy. "Now who's Mrs. Moffet?" said my husband, driving carefully round the corner. "Oh you know, she used to come with her nerves." "So have a lot of people come with their nerves," he said. "Well, she sometimes brought with her that lady who wears a lot of make-up." "Nope," said Bill. "Oh never mind, it's not important—just good to see she's entertaining that's all."

I was paying attention to the bus in front of us, "Stop and Hail—Travel by Bus," the advertisement on the back read. That's a laugh. We're lucky to see a bus down this neck of the woods, let alone hail one. The bus service was dreadful. They've got a nerve, I thought, as Bill, seeing his opportunity, overtook it. This left my vision clear and I, with interest, watched the different pedestrians, wondering where everybody was off to on a Sunday afternoon. Bet there's not many where we're going, I thought, and felt a little thrill run through me—more nerves than anything else. I'm so glad I persuaded Bill to do the address for me—he's a little love. I bet he's scared stiff.

I looked at his thoughtful expression. He appeared to be concentrating on the road ahead, but I bet his head was full of what he was going to speak about. I shuddered at the thought—glad it's not me! "Are you scared dear?" I said, noticing that he had nicked his ear leaving a small trickle of dried blood. Must wipe that off when we stop. "Not so much scared," said Bill, "But a little apprehensive—it will be my first real address on a platform. I just hope I'm good enough." "Oh, you'll be just fine," I said, "You speak really well and you are all right on a platform, you've done the chairing enough times." "Yes," said Bill, "But you lot were always at the back directing me—they won't be here tonight. We're on our own, kid."

That's true, I thought, when any of us chaired a meeting the rest would sit at the back of the church and gently, with hand signs, let the chairman know if his voice was loud enough for everyone to hear, and we would continue to raise our hands until the right volume was audible to the audience. I never had that problem, but some of the new workers did, and Bill was one of them.

"Look," I said, "Don't worry, I don't suppose it's a very big church—so it won't matter as long as you speak clearly. Now pay attention and watch for the underground station. We turn off there."

My husband was now very alert as we were approaching the area we were making for and being foreign to him, concentration was a must , unless we wished to get lost. "It sure is a long drive," I said, breaking the silence. "Look for a railway bridge—should be along this road somewhere." "O.K.," I answered, "I'm looking," taking into my vision at the same time, an old tramp who was slowly walking along the road with his head bent down, probably looking for cigarette ends. His hair was all straggly, hanging down his back. I wonder when it was last washed, I pondered, as we came closer to him. I stared fascinated at his great long overcoat—pockets all torn, with string coming from his shoulder down to his waist. There must have been at least a mile of string around his middle—poor soul, I thought, now taking a front view as we passed him. I could see now why he had got the string coming from his shoulder—hanging on the front of him he had got what looked like dozens of parcels.

"Oh, ha!" I heard Bill remark, "Isn't that a railway bridge I can see." I turned quickly back, "Looks like it, yes," I confirmed, "That's it." "Fine, it should be the third turning on the right past the bridge," Bill's voice, sounding very satisfied by the achievement of having completed the journey without any hitches, reached my ears.

We passed the bridge just as a train was going overhead. I thought how lucky the passengers on the train were—I love travelling on a train. I saw the first turning, then, focusing my eyes as far as I could, I counted the other two, pointing out to Bill that there was a bus stop practically opposite the turning. We arrived at the bus stop, and looking intently, made out the name of the turning. With great difficulty, I might add, as somebody had painted it in mud all over, leaving only the first few letters barely visible.

"This seems to be it," said Bill, and turned the car into the street. "Odd sort of place," I said, "It's very desolate and hardly a soul around. It looks like a shed—it can't be here." I was looking at the only probable building, which definitely, from the outside, gave the impression of being some sort of large garage. "There's nobody about, I wonder if we are in the right place?" "Well, that's the name of the turning all right," said Bill, "I will go and investigate." My husband stepped out of the car, stretching himself, having sat for the past hour and a half. I watched him look about. Mind you, I thought, we are very early. Bill went closer to the building. It was then I saw the notice board, and from where I was sitting I could make out the words "Spiritualist Church".

Bill came back looking relieved. "Yes, this is it," he said. "I could do with a cup of coffee now—maybe we will get one when we go in—we're about three-quarters of an hour early." "Strange sort of place, isn't it," he retorted. I nodded in agreement, looking through my handbag at the same time. I found the paper tissue I was looking for, made it wet with my tongue, and moved closer to Bill. "What are you doing?" he said, backing away instinctively. "It's O.K.," I laughed, "Just cleaning you up." I rubbed gently, "There that's better, you had blood running down your face."

Bill looked in the driving-mirror thoughtfully, and said as he was staring at his face, "I wonder what kind of reception we shall get." "Oh, they will be spellbound," I said, jokingly, "After all, you're so good looking." My husband grinned at me. "I know," he said, laughing back at me, "They won't be able to resist me. Hang on, here's someone."

I strained my eyes and saw a little lady about five feet high. She had a blue head-scarf tied tightly round her head. I watched her carefully as she picked up a crisp bag that was lying just by the door and saw her pop it into a large brown holdall she was holding. She then produced a large key, and after what seemed ages, which was probably only minutes, she undid at least three locks, using a number of keys that I could see all hanging together on what looked like an enormous key ring.

She disappeared inside the building, but came out again within seconds, this time carrying a large broom. I then watched, fascinated, as she fussily swept all around the entrance. I wondered what she was going to do with the small amount of debris that she had collected. At that moment she looked up and started to walk towards the car. I ducked down. "What's the matter," said Bill, seeing me hiding. "Sh!" I said, "I don't want her to see we've been staring at her." "It's O.K., she's going back." I crept up again and saw her walking back, holding a small piece of cardboard in her hand. She then swept the little pile of dirt on to the card, which took two attempts, and then went back into the church. "We'll give her a few minutes," I said, "Then go in."

My husband thoughtfully put his cigarette out into the over-full ash-tray which, I might add, held mostly the remains of my tipped-ends. I was pleased to note that people did indeed live in this part of the world, as I saw a few ladies quickly making their way to the church. I couldn't help smiling on seeing an elderly couple deep in conversation—that is to say the lady appeared to be laying down the riot act to her poor defensive partner, who had probably heard her moans throughout his married life. Yet he, like so many in his position, would be completely lost without his domineering partner.

Bill broke my thoughts, bringing me back with a start as he opened the car door. I pulled myself out and noted with pleasure that my nice new suit had not creased. I patted my hair hoping that it had kept in place. It should have—that new hair spray I bought wasn't all that cheap. I crossed over to the church, leaving Bill to lock the car door, and I took a peep inside, but was disappointed for my view was restricted by some sort of screen—so all I could see were notices plastered all over it. I waited until my husband joined me and we went in together—being greeted almost immediately by the little lady on whom we had been spying earlier. She shook our hands warmly and led us past the rows of chairs, which looked and smelt very old. I took note of the high rostrum as we stopped whilst a door was opened adjacent to the altar.

We were then ushered in and found ourselves inside a tiny room which contained a very old cooker in the corner by a window, where ancient lace curtains hung from a wire. I noted that the wire had been stretched well past its intended length and the lace was entwined amongst the bare springs. That will make it difficult to take down, I thought—no wonder it's so grubby.

"Sit down my dears," said the little lady. We were shown a couple of upright chairs by our chaperone. "I'll be with you in a minute." She then promptly left us. I looked at Bill, who was studying the tiny room intently. "I don't think I like it here very much," I whispered to him. "I can't say that I'm over keen," my husband answered, "Still, not much we can do about it now is there?"

As he spoke the door opened and once again the little lady entered, only this time she introduced us to the organist who, in my opinion, looked strangely foreboding. "Any special hymns you would like," she asked us. Yet, before giving us a chance to answer, proceeded to slide the large numbers on to the hymn board. "I've chosen these for you," she said, handing me a piece of paper, "But if you like I will change them—although I'm sure these will do," she rattled on—explaining that she knew the congregation and therefore what was best for them. My husband said, "They will do nicely."

I never uttered a word. I was too busy looking at the most peculiar hat the organist had upon her head. I couldn't make out if it was a man's beret or not—it certainly looked odd—navy blue in colour, and pulled down one side, covering the left part of her head completely. A mother-of-pearl hat-pin was stuck just above her ear and by the band of the beret two large plume feathers of pink were perched, giving one the impression that they were growing out of her head. I watched her as she put the last couple of numbers on the board, and without another word left the room.

"Well, did you have a good journey?" our chaperon enquired. "Rather a long one," I replied, hoping by my tone this would inspire that much welcomed hot drink. I was quickly disillusioned, however, when she answered by saying, "That's good, now let me tell you that we are a small church and therefore can't pay more than ten shillings for your expenses—so if you sign here," she gave Bill a small receipt book, "I can get all this done with before we start." My husband signed his name. "Saves an awful lot of time afterwards," she said, handing Bill an old torn ten shilling note, "We like to get away promptly."

That, I thought, very disgruntled, means no drink for us. Ah well, water never hurt anyone—good job, for that was going to be the limit of our refreshment. I could tell that this was being made very plain. I wonder they ever get mediums to serve them, I thought.

"Well," she interrupted my thoughts, "Nearly time now, who's to do the address, you dearie?" She was looking at Bill, who nodded to her. "Good, well we like at least twenty-five minutes, preferably longer." I mentally groaned. Poor Bill, he'll never manage. Her voice droned on—"Yes, Sunday meetings are of worship and prayer, so we like to cut down on the clairvoyance and give the congregation teachings from the philosophy of Spirit, it's good for them." I felt like saying exactly what I thought, but controlled myself. I glanced at my poor husband who looked absolutely petrified. His very first address—and I had to bring him here. If only I had known. But it was all too late.

"Give me your hands," I heard her saying, and the next moment, whilst holding our hands up high as though we were playing a game of ring-a-ring-of-roses, in a very loud voice was calling up the Spirit world before the service. I wondered what was coming next. This was all so foreign to us and, I must say, extremely comical. It took great control on my part not to explode with laughter—"Amen," she concluded.

"Right, now you," she looked at Bill, "To the right of me on the platform and your wife on the left." She took hold of my husband pushing him in front of her, at the same time directing me to get behind. "Off you go," she said to Bill, as she gave him a push, and out of the door we came like soldiers in single file. As the door opened the organist began to play. She should have been playing the conga, I thought, as we climbed down the stairs on to the platform.

We each in turn sat solemnly down. I bowed my head—Ah well, here we go. God give us strength. I felt that I was at a funeral service—not in a bright, happy, warm spiritualist church that had been our upbringing. This was so unbelievable that unless I had witnessed the past minutes I would never have believed it. The chairlady stood up and hastily introduced us, then gave out the number of the first hymn. "Everybody stand," she commanded. *O Worship the King,* a loud voice could be heard singing from the back of the church. The organist stopped and turned, staring disapprovingly at the place where the noise had came from. "We'll start again—introduction at the first line, please," she said, emphasising the word "please."

The music started again and everybody waited whilst the first notes were played. The organist then turned towards the congregation and nodded her head—and we all managed to start together. At the beginning of each verse it was like a game as we took a deep breath and waited for her note of command. This continued throughout the hymn, leaving the congregation completely exhausted. I sat down thankfully, very aware of an uncomfortable sore throat. I was relieved to see a tumbler of water on a little shelf in front of me. I drank it down in three quick gulps thirstily. I wiped my wet lips, keeping my head well down, so that the congregation could not see me using the back of my hand, as I had forgotten to bring any tissues with me.

I listened to our chairlady's voice addressing the congregation. "So, if you will pay your subscription fees to Mrs. Turtle after the service, thank you. Now Mr. Macey, our brother, will inspire us all," she said, looking round at Bill, and promptly sat down.

My husband stood up—silence, not a word. It seemed like eternity—probably only seconds really. During this time the audience were fidgeting—getting themselves as comfortable as was possible on the hard chairs that were provided. I heard a nervous cough coming from Bill, followed by the noise of water being swallowed. I watched him looking out at the odd array of the human race, knowing full well that he was unaware at that present moment, for he was struggling for control, waiting patiently for inspiration.

To my relief he began—clear, distinct words. I listened intently, focusing my eyes on a butterfly that had managed to find its way into the gloomy building, and which was circling above a young lady who was sitting at the back of the church. As I watched its delicate wings fluttering, I suddenly became aware of my husband's voice—which was beginning to sound louder and louder with each word. That's odd, I thought, unlike Bill. I quickly glanced across at him as the volume of his voice began to fill the little hall. I couldn't see his face properly—just one side—which, by the colour, was turning beetroot red. I panicked. Whatever was wrong. By this time he was practically shouting.

Some of the congregation started coughing nervously—others pretended not to notice, but Bill continued on, seeming to be unaware of the awful racket he was making. I took another look, noticing that the veins on his neck were standing out quite dramatically due to the strain. Then, only then, did the penny drop as to what was happening. The chairlady was the culprit. She was sitting next to Bill, with her eyes closed, but her hands were upturned on her lap and she was raising them higher and higher—supposedly giving my husband power, but as far as Bill was concerned the raising of hands meant speak louder. We had learnt this in our early development circle days.

Poor Bill, he must be beside himself—thinking that he was addressing deaf mutes. I must try and stop him, I thought, before he does himself an injury. I saw beads of sweat forming tiny patterns on his forehead. I coughed—the shouting continued—I coughed again, this time louder. My husband's voice wavered. He had heard me. I coughed once more. Yes, he had received my message, thank God!

"I'll leave these thoughts with you all," he shouted, "Thank you." A deathly silence prevailed. Many could be heard taking deep breaths of relief. The chairlady rose slowly from her seat, gathering her composure. She cleared her throat politely. "We will now continue our service, singing together, the next hymn—remain seated," she said all in one sentence. The organist began the introduction and, as before, nodded to the congregation to start, having by this time already dared them not to start before cue. We began as the music solemnly played. I prepared myself as all eyes appeared to be on me instead of their hymn books.

One lady in the front row, with an enormous great pair of shaped glasses that were sitting half-way down her nose, fascinated me. The frames were covered in diamante. Our eyes met, and she smiled sweetly at me. I put my head down, mentally I spoke to my Spirit friends—help me, inspire me, I pleaded.

The music had stopped. I heard my name and the words, "Should you be spoken to, speak up clearly so that our Spirit friends will hear." I stood up slowly. I acknowledged the chairlady as I did so. I rubbed my hands together, aware that the butterfly had by now found a window and was trying to find an exit, making tiny taps against the window pane. Funny how clairvoyance always gives immediate attention from the congregation. All eyes were upon me, wondering probably what kind of demonstration they were going to witness after experiencing over twenty minutes of an ear-shattering speaker. Oh well, here goes. "I want to come to you, dear—no dear, not you," I said, as a lady put her hand up, "You dear, that's right, you with the brown coat and glasses." Oh dear, it's going to be one of those days, as three people along the same row, in unison said, "Do you mean me?"

I struggled on, demonstrating my gifts to the very best of my ability. This church service has to go down in history, I mentally thought as I was describing a Spirit named Albert to an eager recipient, and I could not believe my ears when, to my horror, she hotly retorted, "That's my old man! You can send him back, never was any good, so there's no point in him trying to get round me now," amid hushed giggles.

I continued on—thankful to hear the chairlady telling me that time was up. I, like Bill, sat down exhausted. If this be the life of a working medium—well who knows what is in store—this being just the beginning of life behind the scenes of spiritualism. We left that little church with mixed feelings—part of us laughing fit to bust at the extremely funny antics of my husband—and the other wondering whether we would ever be invited to work for them again. But if we thought that was funny, it was nothing to what we were yet to experience.

OH SIR, NOT THE TROUSERS

"Why not give it a try," said the agency girl, persuasively. "Well, if you think I can do it," I answered hesitantly. "Of course you can—it's all figure work and that is what you are used to. It's good money too, don't forget that." I smiled at the fair-haired pretty young girl who was so anxious to get me placed in a position and, at the same time, receive commission should I be accepted by the company to whom she proposed sending me. "O.K.," I said, taking the card she had written out, "I'll give it a try." "You'll be fine," she answered, as I made my way out of the office. "I hope you are right," I replied.

Holding the yellow card in my hand, I arrived at the premises stated. I went to the enquiry office, which was just inside the factory gate, and a friendly voice, said, "Can I help you?" Looking at me through the glass partitioned window was a tall, largely built, middle-aged gentleman. I handed him my introductory card. "Branshaw," he said, "That's who you want young lady. I'll give his secretary a buzz for you—take a seat, I won't be long." With that he closed the window.

I sat down on one of the vacant leather upholstered chairs, feeling very desolate and alone. I picked up a magazine from the neat pile arranged on the glass table. I half-heartedly flicked through the pages and saw it contained information on the products produced by this engineering company. If all works out, I thought, I will be a small part of this big combine. I was most impressed to see how neat and clinical the shop floors looked.

The door opened. "Are you waiting to see Mr. Branshaw," a young girl asked me. I nodded to the youngster who looked as if she had only just left school. "Come along with me," she said importantly. I followed obediently. We went through a large building adjacent to the office we had just left and entered a very nicely decorated reception area. In the centre was a wide staircase up which my chaperon quickly climbed. I followed a little slower—counting the steps as I did so—and on arriving at the top noted there were twenty-one in all. We walked along a carpeted corridor. On one side you could hear the noise of the typewriters coming from the many small offices that we passed.

"Here we are," said my little friend, stopping at a door marked Managing Director—T. M. Branshaw, which words were boldly engraved in large gold letters. T. M. Branshaw—I wonder what the initials stand for, I thought, but before I had time to think about possible names, I was ushered in the room hurriedly. "Mrs. Macey to see you, sir," said the girl in a voice which seemed a little afraid. She stood by the door waiting to be dismissed, "Thank you, Julie, that will be all." With that she closed the door quietly and left.

I stood uncertainly for a few moments, waiting to be given permission to be seated. I took a quick look at the man before me.

He's not to be taken lightly—that's for sure, I thought. He didn't look at all a friendly type. "Do be seated," he interrupted my thoughts. I took the chair which was placed before his desk. The man before me studied my agency card thoughtfully, and then in a clear school-masterly voice said, "Have you ever done stock control." Before giving me the oportunity to answer, he continued, "Only it is important that I have someone who can be left to do the job accurately and without supervision." "No," I replied, "I haven't done stock control before, only wages and a little book-keeping." I wasn't in the least bothered whether I got the job or not and therefore decided to be quite honest with him. I could just imagine what a stickler he would be with regard to rules and regulations. I needed a job, that was true, but the days of yes sir, no sir, were over as far as I was concerned.

"Book-keeping," he said, interestedly. I nodded. "Well now, you shouldn't have any trouble with this particular job. Of course, you will not be on your own to begin with. Would you like to give it a try? I'm sure you will fit in quite nicely here."

Again he gave me no chance to answer before he began to inform me of the salary I could expect, which I must say sounded very tempting. The hours were also extremely good. "When could you start?" he asked. I thought for a moment and decided that I could do a lot worse. "Next Monday," I said, "If that is suitable to you." "Good, I'll expect you at nine o'clock sharp. He stood up—the interview was over. He picked up the internal telephone and asked Julie, who was at the other end, if she would kindly show me out. With that he promptly turned back to the many papers on his desk and appeared to be completely absorbed in them—seemingly ignoring my presence.

I was relieved when Julie arrived to show me out. We left Mr. Branshaw's office quickly. Once outside my young friend said to me, "Well, are you going to join us?" "Yes," I replied. "Oh good," she said happily, "We could do with some new faces here." "Why's that?" I said. "Well," she answered, "Everybody seems so stuffy here." "And you like a bit of fun now and again," I replied. She looked at me with a thoughtful expression. "We used to at school—in between lessons, of course, but here you can only have a laugh when I pop into the sales office. It's great there, but this lot," she indicates with her eyes—"They are all a bit snobby."

I grinned at her. "What makes you think that I'm any different?" She looked carefully at me. "Oh, you can see you're not like them." "I'm very pleased to know that," I said, but wondering at the same time what sort of impression I must be giving her.

"Do you know where you will be working—I mean in what office." "I'm afraid not," I said, "Mr. Branshaw didn't disclose that information." Julie made a funny face at the mention of his name. "Yes, he is a bit of a horror—to be honest he frightens the life out of me, but you get used to him after a time." "Never mind," I said, sympathetically, "It's only because you're the junior." "Yes, you're right there—I'm at everybody's beck and call." She spoke in such a miserable voice that for one moment I wanted to give her a hug.

I remembered my own far off junior days when I was in the same position. "It will only last until the next new junior arrives," I said, trying to cheer her up, "Suddenly everything will change and when you start giving the orders you will forget how you suffered. Anyway, I will be doing stock control—have you any idea where that will be?" "You lucky old thing," said Julie, "That's in the sales office in Mr. Wilson's section." "What's he like," I asked. "Well, actually he's not a bad type, he can be funny at times, but he can also be good for a laugh when he's in the mood, but you'll love Francis, he's smashing!" "Good-looking?" I interrupted her. "Oh no, nothing like that," she replied, "He's just good fun and I bet they sit you next to him because I think he has something to do with stock."

We had, by now, reached the reception area and stood talking by the door. "Well, see you on Monday," I said. "By the way, what's your name?" asked Julie. "Sheila," I answered her. "Mine's Julie." "Yes, I gathered that, " I said, "When Mr. Branshaw telephoned you." I heard a young female voice calling out Julie's name. "I'd better go," she said anxiously, as her name was repeated again. "Right," I said, "See you." "Yes, smashing," she said, scampering up the stairs two at a time. I left the building with mixed feelings—I had now committed myself to the new job. I knew that at the very least I would have to give it a try.

I arrived on good time the following Monday morning and was greeted by a most peculiar looking man. I was fascinated by the fact that he had not one hair on his head. Mind you, he didn't look a bit like Yul Bryner. "Pleased to meet you," said the man, "I'm Mr. Wilson. Follow me and I'll show you where you will be sitting. I've put you next to Mr. Greenapple." I quickly followed him. For his age Mr. Wilson was very agile. He was tall and slim and I should think somewhere around his middle fifties. I couldn't help staring at the back of his head as we hurried along the now familiar corridor. You could see where he had shaved it from the tell-tale razor marks.

"Here we are, Francis, meet Mrs. Macey." He turned towards me, What's your christian name by the way?" "Sheila," I said, taking the hand of a very feminine-looking young male. "How do you do," he said, with a voice that matched his looks. I smiled at him. "Very well, thank you." "So I'm to have company at last," said Francis, "God, its been awful. You really can't imagine how bad its been—I've not had a moment to myself." He looked down at me—for he was very tall. "Don't worry about it, love," he said to me, "I'll show you the ropes." "Thanks," I replied, taking the seat behind my appointed desk.

On being seated I took note of my surroundings. Immediately in front of me was a large assortment of heavy ledgers. These blocked my view of the rest of the office. I leaned over to one side to get a clearer picture of the long open-planned office and the many bodies who were beginning to arrive. I must say they didn't look over-enthusiastic about the prospect of starting another week's work. I turned back to the job in hand, not feeling terribly keen myself and longing to turn tail and run.

"Now my dear," said Francis, "Let's get you started." With a loud clatter he placed some of the heavy ledgers on my desk. I became very involved with my work. First there was adding and then subtracting and I felt like a calculator as the figures danced before my eyes. On that first morning the whole nature of the work made little sense to me and my poor brain felt most befuddled. Luckily, within a few short weeks, I mastered the whole set up and found each day so much easier than the last.

Francis was indeed much fun to have around—just as young Julie had told me when I came for my interview. I found myself in uncontrollable laughter many times at his antics. I also made friends with the rest of the office crew and became happy in my employment. The weeks flew by into months and I gained valuable experience in the art of stock-taking. In fact, I became so accustomed to the work that I could afford to take more interest in my fellow workers. There was only three of us employed on the stock section. Francis, myself and Mr. Wilson, who wasn't too bad to work for although at times he could be awkward. When things weren't to his liking he was not above showing his annoyance by shouting and generally making life miserable for those who crossed his path. On the whole I got on pretty well with him.

Then there was Lucy! She worked for the salesmen and mostly typed out orders as they took them over the telephones, which were placed on practically every desk, there being two on almost every one—on some, even three. On occasions, when they all decided to ring at the same time, there was an almighty din and you couldn't hear yourself speak. Lucy got on fine with everybody provided you didn't rush her. She would sit typing away quite happily and sometimes would take it into her head to give us all a rendering of some recent tune that she had heard on the hit parade. At times, what with the telephones all going mad, and Lucy's unmusical voice, some ear-plugs would have been gratefully received. Lucy, however, would sing away, really happy in her work, unaware of the noise she was making.

She would at times wear the most extraordinary outfits. She was of slight build and about five feet tall. At times she looked like a fashion model who had crossed with the wrong designer, and her choice of colour left a lot to be desired. It was immaterial to her whether they suited or not. She was quite popular with everybody until she had one of her tantrums then all hell let loose. Usually, it was started by one of the salesmen who needed an order typed urgently—one that had probably been taken earlier in the day.

"What do you think I've been doing all day," would be the first outburst, followed by, "You expect me to do everything in this damned office." Then in a flood of tears she would rush out of the office leaving the salesman, who started the whole thing off, looking bewildered, uneasy and cross. He was also aware of the fact that because he had upset her he would now have to wait much longer for his order.

Lucy worked for three salesmen in all. Bob, who had just been the instigator of her outburst—a very friendly fellow, who definitely intended going places in his career. He was keen and aggressive in his selling approach and gave his all to the job in hand. He was also a handsome man. His face still, as yet, showed early years of youth. He had dark, almost black hair, which was complimented by lovely rich brown eyes. Although to me he appeared almost too young, he had recently married.

Peter, the youngest salesman at eighteen, was very serious in his approach to life, and this appeared to make him seem much older. I sometimes watched him from behind my ledgers and admired the way he enjoyed his work. He, also, was out to impress the boss with as many orders as he could possibly achieve each day. Nevertheless, he was a thoroughly nice sort of chap and was well liked by the department.

Graham was the eldest of the three, also very keen and ambitious. He was for ever rushing backwards and forwards from one office to another. As he was in charge of his section he of course had added responsibilities and I was amazed how he managed to diplomatically sort out the many problems which arose—one of them being the sudden outbursts of Lucy. Somehow or other he had the knack of keeping peace all round. Poor Graham lived on his nerves, however, and I felt sorry for him when on occasions he came to me for lists of stock figures. I would try to calm him down, but invariably he would just laugh at me in the nicest way and tell me to mind my own business. It was a great shame as he was definitely the target for ulcer trouble in the not too far distant future.

Hilda was the oldest inhabitant of the office—not in age, but length of service. She had spent many years in the department and had gained much respect from the rest of her colleagues by virtue of the fact that she was a mine of information and there were very few events that she couldn't come up with. She was roughly in her middle twenties, rather a nice-looking girl, and very neat in her manner of dress. Not at all like Lucy. Hilda preferred to wear quiet colours and her clothes matched her personality. Hilda was also most popular with the department and enjoyed her work.

This, then, was where I spent most of my days, and my colleagues brought a great deal of laughter into my working life, and earning our daily bread wasn't too much of a chore. One day Francis came into the office and said to me, "You had better be on your best behaviour today," ruffling my hair as was his usual habit. I'm sure he did this as he towered over me and it gave him a sense of power.

"Why, who's coming?" I said, as I tried to straighten my hair. I was already feeling a bit put out as I had experienced yet another bad morning on the train and my nerves felt jagged. "Now don't get all upset with me," said Francis in a plaintive voice, "We've got the top brass coming from the parent company plus all the reps from our other companies. Won't it be fun! I can't wait," he said enthusiastically, clapping his hands happily.

"Oh, you are funny, Francis," I said, laughing at him. One couldn't be cross with him for long—he was such a good natured chap and his feminine actions were really quite endearing. I sat down and began my work. I was quite looking forward to the promised visitors—anything in the change of routine was welcome. I noticed it brought a sense of excitement in an otherwise ordinary day.

Just about half-past-ten that morning the procession arrived, headed by old Branshaw himself, Francis dug me in the ribs making me cry out. Mr. Branshaw gave me a disapproving look. "See what you've done now," I said, between clenched teeth. It didn't make any difference to my attacker, he thought it was very funny. "Oh lovey," he said, "You did make a noise, I bet old Branshaw nearly had a fit." "Now pack it up," I said to him good naturedly, "Otherwise I'll be out of a job."

I suppose in all there were about twenty people in the so called party of diplomats. They slowly made their way to each section, some taking notes, others listening with apparent interest to questions asked of employees. I could see that our managing director was having a whale of a time. His voice could be heard very clearly in the unfamiliar quiet office. All heads were down in the height of industry. They finally made their way to our section. It seemed as if many faces were looking down at me as I showed them my ledgers. Mr Wilson, as head of the section, was explaining the procedure I undertook.

After what appeared to an incredible length of time the party finally left, making a considerable amount of noise as they made their way to the exit. You could feel the relief of tension as the door closed behind the last body. We all let out a great sigh and relaxed, chattering non-stop with each other.

"Well that's over," I said, turning to Francis. Francis, however, was not in the slightest bit interested in me, and was looking in amazement at the gentleman who was fast approaching my desk. I had recognised him amongst the now departed party. He stopped at my side and bent his head towards mine. Francis, I noted, was intent on not missing a thing.

"Forgive me," was the first words the man said, in a smooth clear cut voice, "But aren't you Mrs. Macey the medium? I was shocked that he remembered me—the office was the last place I wished to be recognised as a medium. From past experience I had decided to keep my outside activities to myself. Once people knew that I had this gift I had no chance to relax and they always expected me to give readings.

"Yes I am," I replied. "I thought you were. Well this is a surprise, fancy coming all the way to a works seminar to find you here. The wife and I were only speaking about you the other evening." I groaned inwardly. If only he would speak a little quieter. Already he had caused a considerable stir by his words. "Yes," he continued, "That was some meeting—we enjoyed it immensely. Have you been here long?" he enquired, "Only I don't remember seeing you on my last visit to the company."

By this time I was more than a little embarrassed and asked if he shouldn't be getting back to his party. "O.K.," he said, "I get the message—mum's the word," as he put his finger to his lips. "Not really," I replied, "It's just that I haven't told my colleagues what I am." "Oh sorry," he said apologetically, "Just the shock of seeing you here. Hope I haven't put my foot in it." He had done that all right. It was going to be murder from now on and I knew that things would be vastly different in the sales office. "Well, hope to see you soon, maybe on my next visit." He shook my hand warmly then hurriedly left the room.

"What's all this about then," said Francis, as he eyed me suspiciously, "You one of them?" "One of what," I said hotly. "A witch." I laughed out loud. "You are, aren't you?" he said, "I knew there was something odd about you all along." "Don't tell such fibs," I interrupted him before anything more was said, "I'm a medium, that's all, nothing odd about that, nothing at all, and you would never have known if I hadn't been recognised." "Where do you keep your broomstick?" he said playfully, not taking any heed of what I was saying. "Here gang," he directed his attention to the rest of the office, "We've got a witchy-poo with us," he said, as he giggled away to himself. "Stop it Francis," I cried, "Or I'll turn you into a frog if you're not careful—so behave." "Cor, I do believe you could," he said, giving me a pretence frightened look.

It took much control on my part before Francis finally accepted the idea of my being a medium. He made fun of me unmercifully. As I predicted, things were never the same after that fateful day. Once it became common knowledge around the building that a medium was amongst their number I became a target for much friendly teasing. I took this all in good humour—knowing them all so well, I really didn't mind.

It must have been roughly eighteen months later that I was approached by Mr. Branshaw's secretary. We had never had a great deal in common—to be honest I didn't much like her attitude. She always gave the impression of looking down on people and being the managing director's secretary thought she was a cut above the rest of us. Not so long back I had put her in her place when she upset one of the younger members of the staff. So I was more than a little surprised when she stopped me in the corridor as I made my way to get some stock sheets from the foreman in the factory. I enjoyed that part of my job. It gave me a chance to meet the manual workers and they were such a cheery lot. "Good morning," they would shout at me above the noise of the heavy machinery. They always had some little joke to make me smile. "Have you heard the one about . . ." they would say, giving me some story, and I would pretend to look surprised and a little shocked, which never failed to make their day.

"Sheila, can I have a word." "Certainly," I said, making my way into a small but attractive looking room. There were two desks, nicely spaced out, one being by a window, and at which my addresser sat. The other was placed a little further away and this was for young Julie's use. At that moment she was missing—probably on some urgent message. Poor Julie, she was still the junior. I still had a soft spot for her and often found myself defending her when she was in trouble over something or other.

"What's up?" I said, turning my attention to the girl in front of me. A somewhat beautiful face looked keenly at me. She could be most attractive, I thought, if only she didn't have such snobby ways. "I'm very worried about Mr. Branshaw," she said quickly, "And I was wondering if you could help." "In what way?" I said, astonished by the question, for I couldn't imagine that I would be of any help. Mr. Branshaw was a law unto himself and apart from the odd query regarding figures for my stock control, I mostly stayed out of his way. To be perfectly honest I had never cared much for the man and therefore paid little attention to him.

Tina looked anxiously towards the office door, not wanting to be overheard. "He's in terrible pain," she said worriedly, "I've been concerned about him all week." "It's his back," she continued, still keeping a wary eye out towards the door, "I'm afraid for him—something must be done or he is sure to crack under the strain." "As bad as that," I said, "I am sorry, but what can I do?"

"Well, I do know what you do out of office hours—I mean, I've heard," she said with a red face, "Alan has told me lots of things about you." "Alan," I said "Who's he?" "You remember, the man who recognised you sometime back when the management had a general meeting. I have to telephone him quite a lot about business for Mr. Branshaw and that's how I found out." she said, "Can you do anything for him? He really is in a shocking state."

"Come on Tina, do you think for one minute old Branshaw's going to let me touch him," I asked. I shivered at the prospect. I was able to say no to anybody but him. "Please try," said Tina, "He's not so bad and he can't go on much longer as he is."

I wondered what Mr. Branshaw's thoughts would have been had he heard his secretary pleading on his behalf. Lucky man to have such devotion, I reflected. "Look, let me think it over and if I do decide you'll have to make the first approach, O.K.?" Tina shook her head, "Oh no, I couldn't possibly—it's got to come from you—after all you know what you are talking about and will be able to put it over much better than I." "You're not asking for much are you—I must be crazy even to consider it." "Please," she said, in a persuasive voice. "I'll see—that's all I'm saying for now." With that I left the small office and quickly returned to the hustle and bustle of the sales office.

"You've been simply ages," I was greeted by Francis accusingly, "Where have you been all this time?" I put my finger to my nose. "That's my business," I said mysteriously. "It's not fair," said my friend, "You've got something up your sleeve." "Well, that's my secret and that's how it is going to be," I said, as I got on with my work.

I found it extremely difficult to sit and concentrate. I couldn't get Theodore Branshaw off my mind. How on earth was I going to approach him. He was not a very agreeable type of chap at the best of times. In pain, he would probably be a lot worse. I do get them, I complained to myself, although I knew full well that I should have to try. If only my husband were here—he would make me feel a little more confident. Bill's approach, I knew, would be direct, giving the patient little time to think. Maybe that's the way to do it, I thought, don't give him time to consider.

Mr. Branshaw, I rehearsed in my brain, I understand that you are in great pain—have you ever thought about healing—only my husband and I do practice the gift and I feel sure I could alleviate some of your pain. Yes, that's what I'll do, I decided. But finding the courage was another matter altogether. I sat at my desk going over and over what I was going to say.

"You've gone all quiet on me," said Francis, "What's up—something on your mind? You've been like that since you came back from the other office." I wanted so much to confide in someone, but knew that dear Francis was hardly the person. "Look, I've got a problem at the moment which I can't disclose. Please understand. It's not that I don't respect your trust." "All right duckie, I won't say another word," he said, "Honest." "Thanks," I replied, gratefully, as I turned back to my inner thoughts.

It was almost eleven-thirty when I eventually decided to make the approach, having built within me a sense of bravado but already accepted my fate that things would go wrong. Just knowing the man's temperament was off-putting and I knew he could easily send me packing. I stood up slowly, stretching my legs as I did so. It's now or never, I thought. With that I made my way out of the office, my eyes fixed firmly ahead. I dared not stop as I knew I would change my mind. I made my way slowly along the carpeted corridor. I could feel my heart racing, making me take short, sharp breaths of air. As I grew nearer to Mr. Branshaw's office I found myself having to stop to take a few deep breaths. This is ridiculous, I reproached myself, whatever next. After all you are going to help him, not ask for a rise. Now calm down and get on with it.

Having scolded myself, upon reaching the dreaded door, I knocked, hoping against hope that the office would be empty. I knocked very faintly once again and stood there for a few seconds. "Good, it's empty," I said with a sigh of relief. But it wasn't. "Come in," said a disgruntled voice. Oh God, I thought, completely forgetting my well-rehearsed lines. It was too late. I was in the room.

"Well," Branshaw demanded, not looking up from the papers before him as he worked at his large desk. I have never seen so many papers and computer tabs in my life—there wasn't a space to be seen. I coughed politely. "Can I have a word with you, sir," I said, trying to sound natural and failing dismally. He looked up from the large sheet of figures in front of him. Pain had certainly had its effect. Although he was not a particularly good-looking man, he did have a nice strong jaw line, deep-set hazel eyes and a good mop of rich brown hair. Apart from his overweight body he really didn't do so bad as far as looks were concerned. At that moment, however, his face was visibly lined with constant pain making him look years older than he probably was.

When I spoke the words just came tumbling out—nothing like I had decided. He just sat there staring at me as I was speaking. "So if you will allow me, I feel sure I may be able to help." I stopped then—suddenly finding nothing more to say. The silence was unnerving and I wasn't sure what I should do—so as the lesser of two evils I remained where I was.

After an incredible length of time he finally spoke. "Can you do something for me?" he asked. He has accepted, I immediately thought. That's one hurdle over. "I'm in terrible pain." "Well, I would like to give it a try if you'll let me," I answered. "I must confess I know very little about these matters," said Mr. Branshaw, "Although I have heard stories." "Right, I'll just go and wash my hands. In the meantime if you could sit sideways on this chair," I said, as I placed an upright seat in front of his desk, "I'll see what I can do for you." With that I left the room, feeling very pleased with myself for having made the approach and talking him into letting me give him healing.

I hurriedly made my way to the washroom. I was pleased to find it empty as I had so much on my mind and didn't want to be distracted by idle chatter. I washed my hands thoroughly and took a quick look in the mirror and saw my very flushed face. Understandable, I thought. It wasn't every day one had a chance to give healing to their boss. "This is it then," I said, as I left the ladies' room, feeling the quickening of my heart.

It took me about a minute to get back. The words Managing Director made my heart miss a beat for a second, but I swallowed, took a deep breath, and this time entered without knocking. I was completely staggered by the scene. I stood rigid in a state of shock. Oh, my God, this is awful. Thank goodness he can't see my face. The picture before me was Theodore M. Branshaw, sitting sideways on the chair as requested, with his trousers draped around his ankles and his underpants pulled well down giving me a view of his cheeks spread out all over the seat.

My first reaction was to shout out, but I controlled the desire knowing full well that if I showed any signs of panic it would make my patient feel as embarrassed as I was. For a few seconds I just stood there, trying desperately to hold back the hysteria that was welling up inside me. Nobody knew I was here, I hadn't even told Tina of my decision. I wasn't sure what I would have done if anybody had walked in at that precise moment.

I nervously looked back at the door. Yes, it was firmly shut. "The pain is at its worst right here," said Mr. Branshaw, pointing with his finger towards the lower part of his lumber region. "Umm," I said, trying to sound very efficient as if this sort of caper happened to me every day. My stomach was beginning to ache something awful as I held back my laughter.

I laid my hands on his exposed body, finding my fingers sinking in to the fleshy mounds of fat. I tried very hard not to allow personal thoughts invade my mind, as I had been taught, but it was no good. Those damn trousers were the culprit—all I could see out of the corner of my eyes were them around his ankles.

Then it happened—the thing I dreaded most. There was a commotion outside the door and then a slight tap. Mr. Branshaw looked up painfully on hearing the disturbance, but due to his disability was unable to stand quickly enough in order to pull up his pants and trousers. Not realizing the implications I, in a panic, bent down to help—and that is how we were caught as the door swung open. The picture we must have made could not have left anything to anyone's imagination, but worse was to come.

Children's giggles could be heard coming from the open doorway. Today of all days the personnel officer was on one of his work experience tours. I fled from the office, sending the children all over the place, and noting the complete look of disbelief on the face of the officer. I never did see Mr. Branshaw after that day. Tina said he had decided to go sick after all. A few weeks later she told me that she had been informed of his transfer. "Strange," she said, "There was never a mention of him going." I smiled, "Oh well, at least I don't have to approach him after all." "No," said Tina, thoughtfully, "But many thanks anyway."

I left Tina's office with my secret more-or-less intact. Poor old Branshaw—I never did find out if I did him any good. I couldn't help chuckling to myself when Francis stopped me a few weeks later as I was making my way out of the office—"You'll never guess what I've just heard about our Theodore." "No Francis," I replied, "I could never guess in a thousand years."

A HAUNTING WE MUST GO

As I walked up my garden pathway I could hear the telephone ringing. I was returning from the local supermarket. This particular task had taken me much longer than I had anticipated—being caused by the fact that as I carried out my carefully packed carrier-bags one of the handles snapped and my shopping merrily made its way towards the road. I managed to retrieve the offending articles and repack them, but decided rather than risk the other carrier bag giving way I would carry them both in my arms. By the time I arrived home my arms felt as if they had been pulled out of their sockets.

"Hold on," I shouted at no one and nothing in particular, as I attempted to perform the simple job of putting the key in the lock. Suddenly the door swung open and I practically threw my purchases on to the hall floor. I hurriedly picked up the telphone and said, "Hello, can I help you?"

"Oh, good afternoon," said a rather nervous voice at the other end of the line, "Are you the lady," and at this stage the caller coughed, "I mean, do you tell fortunes?" "No," I said, "I am not a fortune-teller, I am a spiritualist medium." "I see," said the voice, "You can tell me where my horse has gone." "I beg your pardon," I said, not at all sure that I had heard her correctly. "My horse has gone," she repeated, "And I thought you could let me know where I could find it."

The speaker was now gaining a little more confidence and went on—"You see I've heard all about you and how clever you are and thought perhaps you could help me." "Well, thank you for the compliment," I replied, "But I am afraid you are under a misapprehension. I'm sorry I can't help you," but as an afterthought added, "How come you managed to lose your horse?"

Tearfully my caller replied, "He went missing from the field last night and I'm so worried about him." "Why don't you contact the local farmers in the area," I asked, "They are sure to be quite helpful. I'm sorry," I said, "But that's about all the help I can offer you," and with that I brought the conversation to a halt. Wishing her good luck, I replaced the receiver.

What an odd request, I thought, I certainly do get them! Still, it was comforting to think that people had that amount of trust in mediumship. Well, I can't afford to waste any more time, I thought, as I picked up the items I had purchased from the supermarket. It took me three journeys backwards and forwards to get all my goods to the kitchen—how I hate putting them away. Tinned stuff on the top shelf, meat in the freezer, potatoes at the bottom of the larder, butter in the fridge and so on.

By this time I realized that I was absolutely parched and must have a cup of coffee. I filled the kettle and flopped on to the kitchen chair whilst waiting for it to boil and thankfully kicked off my shoes. I'm really looking forward to our evening of clairvoyance tonight, I thought, as I leisurely put some instant coffee in my favourite mug and waited for the kettle to boil, they are always so good. The kettle boiled and I poured the boiling water over the coffee and watched the powder froth. The aroma reached my nostrils and smelled most inviting. I sat down and sipped the hot drink appreciatively.

Ring, ring, the telephone began again. "Bother," I said to myself, "The blessed thing never leaves me alone for a minute," "Yes," I said, on picking up the instrument, without first relaying my number, "Who is it?" I knew my voice must have sounded sharp. "Mrs. Macey," came back the reply. "Yes," I said, by now feeling a bit guilty, "What can I do for you?" I made a genuine effort to soften my tone.

"My wife and I are in desperate need of help," said the agitated voice, "We have been almost everywhere and are at the end of our tether." I listened carefully to the well-educated voice which had an accent that appeared to originate from the North Country. "I think our house is haunted—we have experienced so many strange happenings and it's very frightening." He quickened his words as he tried to explain the position to me. "My wife is in a terrible state. We have had the local vicar to the house and he did some peculiar things and we have also contacted a gentleman who is supposed to be able to exorcise evil spirits, but none of it has been of any use." He stopped to take a breath and thereby gave me a chance to speak.

"Look," I said, "Let me take down your name and address, and your telephone number, and I will get back to you." I wrote down the required information. "Please do, urgently," my caller said. "Of course I will," I replied, "As soon as my husband returns home and I am able to discuss the matter with him."

I returned to the kitchen where fortunately my coffee had remained quite hot. "A haunting," I said out loud, "That's exciting, we haven't had one crop up for some time." I remembered our last case. It was quite local to where we lived and was very interesting, and just as in this case, we were asked to investigate. The people concerned had also tried to obtain all sorts of help but to no avail and had turned to us as a last resort.

The event came flooding back to my memory. It concerned a young couple who lived on a very nice estate not far from our own. They had a couple of children, a little boy aged about four years and a small baby of six months. The young mother had been aware of noises coming from the bedrooms of the house, but could not detect from which one—she only knew the sound was real. Mostly it was a young baby's cry which caused her some distress.

Nobody really believed her story until one evening the couple left their children in charge of the wife's brother whilst they attended a party to which they had been invited. They did not leave the house until both children were well and truly asleep and therefore the baby-sitter was able to spend a relaxed evening watching television. All was well for best part of the evening until suddenly he became aware of a baby crying upstairs. He had not been told by his sister of the weird noises she had been experiencing and therefore hurried to the baby's room to check that all was well.

On peering at the baby he was amazed to find that it was still fast asleep and decided that he must have made a mistake and returned to his television programme. However, within minutes, the distinct noise of a crying baby could be heard. This time the man climbed the stairs very quietly—thinking that perhaps the child was having him on. On reaching the landing he followed the whimpering sound into the baby's room. "So it was you," he said, as he went up to the cot. The crying had by now increased and sounded very distressed. Turning on the small bedside light he looked down at the young child and was astonished to see that the babe was very much asleep. The man, still hearing the crying, became alarmed that he fled from the house to the telephone box at the end of the street in order to telephone the parents. He told them what he had heard, but on no account would he go back into the house.

He waited by the front door and later said that he had never been so scared in all his life. Now that proof had been obtained the couple decided to call in professionals to solve the problem. Unfortunately, the noise still went on and they decided to ask my husband and I to look into the matter. We found out about its past inhabitants and then investigated the house.

It was quite an intriguing story. Apparently a young girl had committed suicide in the house many years previously and so we decided to hold a seance to see if we could help her. We arranged to have the sitting late in the evening when all would be quiet—particularly the children. I made myself ready by sitting on a small armchair which had been placed in the bathroom.

Both Bill, my husband, and I, felt an oddness within this small room. It was cold and most definitely uninviting. I shivered as the memory came rushing back to me. However, we did have some marvellous results. Apparently, through my entranced state, the poor girl who had commited suicide told Bill that she was a child herself of some fifteen years. She informed my husband that she had got herself into trouble, and her father, being of a strict

Victorian nature, terrified her. She was therefore unable to tell her parents of her pregnant state and tried to keep her secret through tight clothing for most of her nine-month pregnancy.

After a dreadful row with her father because he told her that she was not doing her share of the housework, in sheer panic she fled into the bathroom and with the clothes-line which served its purpose in wet weather, she tragically ended her short life. My husband asked her why she was now tormenting the people who lived in the house. "But I'm not," she answered, "I am only trying to find my baby. I keep hearing it cry so I know it needs me." "Surely," said my husband, "In your world there must be those who look after such children." "Oh yes they do, it is so beautiful," said the unhappy voice, "But because I ended my own life before its time, and my baby was due to be born, I can only find my child when I call. It hears me and cries, but I can't reach." "Is it because you are on different levels that you cannot reach the baby," asked Bill. "Yes, I think so," came back the reply. "Look," said my husband, "We will see what can be done if you promise not to cause any more disturbances. You must now allow another to use this communication, one who is very learned and kind. I shall ask help for you, go now."

The girl left me and a Spirit guide came and help was asked that the young girl could be shown her baby and given peace to her troubled mind so that she could learn and advance in her spiritual pathway. After that night's seance all the noises stopped and nothing more was heard. We had both been a little frightened about the haunting as we had had little experience of such things, but were, nevertheless, thrilled by our success.

I pulled myself together, coming back to reality. I can't sit here all day dreaming, I've a dinner to get. I washed up my attractive mug, watching the hot water circle round the picture of Mrs. Beeton, who was wearing an apron. I wonder if that girl is anywhere around, I pondered. What a wonderful thing it would be if she could be our guide. As I dried my mug and looked at the picture of Mrs. Beeton I thought how lovely it would be to have her help in the kitchen, but what a shock she would have on seeing the modern kitchens and gadgets of today. My imagination took me back to Mrs. Beeton's day—about the 1850's I thought. How on earth did they survive all that hard work—especially the large meals they prepared. Still, with the pace of life we have to live today, it would be impossible, I thought, making excuses for my lack of enthusiasm.

The rest of my afternoon was filled with household chores and I felt pretty pleased with myself by the time Bill arrived home. Over our evening meal I told him about the telephone call I had had earlier. "What do you think?" I said, biting into a crusty roll. "The man certainly sounded very worried about the problem," I continued. Whilst I was speaking I was pleased to see that the meat pie which I had prepared was vanishing down Bill's stomach. I bet that's just as good as Mrs. Beeton's I kidded myself. "Great pie," said Bill, "It tastes really smashing." It always gave me a thrill when I saw my husband enjoying his meal.

"Well," said Bill, "Did he say what had been happening?" "No, to be honest I never asked. I just said that I would contact him after I had spoken to you." "O.K.," said Bill, "You had better make arrangements for tomorrow evening."

"I don't know," said Bill, "Perhaps one of these days we may have a little time to ourselves." I smiled at him affectionately. "You old softy," I replied, "I do believe you are making a pass at me." He laughed—"Chance would be a fine thing—and by the way woman, that dinner was really smashing. You're improving," he added, "With age." "Why you," I began, but was interrupted by the telephone ringing. "I'll get it," said my spouse, with a wicked grin on his face. "It's that fellow again—I told him that we would be round just after eight o'clock tomorrow night." "Fine," I said, "But come on Bill we had better get ready for tonight or we shall be late." "Right, I'm on my way," I heard Bill shout as he ran up the stairs.

I had washed earlier so all that was left for me to do was to make up my face. As I looked at myself in the mirror I critically examined the lines that were appearing on my face. I pulled the skin tight around my eyes and looked like a Chinaman. I sighed, remembering an experience I had had only the other day. Although the mini-skirt had been around for some time I had only just plucked up courage to wear one when I went to work. It was very plain and a lovely lilac colour and made of a very heavy nylon material which was popular for such dresses at the time. I haven't got a bad pair of legs and felt pretty good in my mini. However, I very soon learnt a cruel lesson that my age was fast creeping up on me.

I was hurrying to catch the 8.30 a.m. train when I became aware of wolf whistles. I couldn't see any other females in sight and I knew that some workmen in the distance were taking an interest in me. It felt good, really good, so I continued walking smartly towards them. On approaching the workmen I daringly gave them a smile, when suddenly my whole world fell apart as the following words were spoken. "Gosh, you'd make a smashing mum." I was shattered. Not so much with what was said, but the silly way I had acted. Still, I said to myself, all things considered you're not so bad for your age—not so good-looking as your sister, she is lovely. Slim, where I was slightly bigger built, and dark curly hair. My hair was over-bleached and therefore not anywhere near as pretty. She also had beautiful brown eyes and mine were in-between—green and grey. Still, I didn't mind, I loved her even though she always looked like my kid sister, but was five years older than myself.

Oh well, I told myself crossly, that's enough of that, Bill will be ready before me at this rate. I took a last look in the mirror and decided that my efforts were quite pleasing. I was wearing a navy blue pleated skirt which I had complimented with a new white blouse. I wasn't too hot on fashion but this combination was just right for me.

"Do you want any more coffee before we go?" I asked Bill. "How are we for time?" came back the reply. "We've got at least half-an-hour to spare." "O.K. then, go ahead, I'll be down in a moment." I went into the kitchen and made the coffee. Bill came into the kitchen tying a knot in his tie. It always intrigued me that most men could manage this so neatly. When I was in the girl guides I regularly lost marks from the patrol leader because of my inability to knot a tie correctly.

"Hey where are you?" said Bill as he clicked his fingers near my face. "Just day-dreaming," I replied. "You look smart," I told Bill as he turned towards me. He was wearing a navy blue blazer and grey slacks. "Do you think so? You are a handsome brute," he said as he looked at his reflection in the mirror. "Pity your hair is turning grey," I laughed. "Where," he said, going close up to the glass. "Come on," I said, "We haven't got time for you to do an inspection."

"I wonder if there will be a full house tonight," I asked Bill. Most evenings of clairvoyance usually did bring the people in and most times you could be sure of a fairly large crowd. "Bill," I said, "Do you think we should get involved with this haunting? I mean they do worry me a little." My husband looked at me in surprise. "To be perfectly honest they scare me to death." "You've got to be kidding," said my husband still looking astonished. "It's true," I replied, "I know they are awfully interesting, but I don't think it's my kind of scene. After that man called this afternoon I found myself going over the last episode—you remember—where the baby kept crying. I know we were lucky enough to clear the problem up, but don't you think that sort of thing should be left to others and not us?"

"Oh come on with you," said my husband, "You are dealing with the Spirit world all the time. You can't possibly be scared, can you?" as he realised that I wasn't having him on. "To be honest," I said, "I don't feel right—there's something odd about that man's voice." "I'll admit," said Bill, "He did sound funny, but I put that down to his concern for his wife." "Oh well, we can't worry about it now—let's get cracking or we are going to be late and we mustn't keep our audience waiting."

I quickly rinsed the cups and put all thoughts of the subject out of my head as I prepared myself for the night's work. We made good time and had time to spare on arrival. As was usual the evening had attracted a large crowd and I watched, from my position at the end of the hall, the people, as they took their seats. I smiled as I eavesdropped on a conversation which two ladies were having. One said, "I always wear a hat deary, it never fails. Isn't that right, Fred?" she said, turning to a funny-looking little man who was sitting on her other side. "She's right," he replied. "Every week without fail—you want to try it sometime!" Well, I thought, if I have anything to do with it she won't get a message tonight.

It is always the same—no matter where you go there are always the message seekers. I could usually pick them out. Great for business though, I mused, they invariably spread the news of the movement on whose ever ears would happen to listen—so I suppose one shouldn't get cross with them.

I turned my attention to an enormous lady who had just entered the hall. Small beads of sweat could be seen quite clearly on her forehead. I watched fascinated as she walked down the centre aisle, her large hips touching the bodies of those who were sitting on the end seats. They automatically leaned away on seeing her large frame. She took a vacant seat on the end of the second from front row and sat heavily down. I swear I saw the legs of the chair bow out on receipt of the heavy load.

I looked at my watch—almost time. A sudden hush stilled the noisy hall. The organist took her seat. I was handed a hymn book by a very red faced man who whispered to me that he would be chairing for me instead of Mrs. Sykes. He then faced the audience. "Good evening, ladies and gentlemen, how nice to see so many of you here tonight. We will begin our service by singing hymn number 105 in the blue book—please be upstanding."

As the music began the introduction, I couldn't help wondering why he specifically said the blue book, for I could see no other. I liked the hymn we were about to sing so I joined the congregation and sang with gusto, in a hearty voice. On hearing my loud voice the congregation also sang with all their might and main and I could feel the vibrations lifting beautifully as we came to the last few lines. Amen. Silence, then a prayer, after which I was introduced.

I heard the chairman tell the audience that should they be spoken to by the medium they should answer quickly and clearly but not feed her with information. I took this remark as being extraordinarily funny—seeing myself as being in some sort of cage. I addressed the audience and laughingly told them that I was on a diet. This caused a ripple of laughter and lifted still more vibrations.

"I would like to come to you, dear," I said. I was drawn to the fat lady who, by this time, was sweating profusely. She answered in a tiny squeaky voice which, for a second, took me aback. "Do you know someone called Snowy in Spirit?" I asked, but before she could answer my head started to go up and down. "Why, it's a large cat. I can see it quite clearly now—it had a funny habit of nudging its head up and down when you stroked it." "Oh how lovely," said the fat lady, her face showing the great affection she had had for the cat, "My Snowy, oh how I have missed him." She mopped her brow as she looked up at me. "You have also got a friend who sends his regards—he says how about a milk stout!"

"No, I can't think who that could be," she answered. "Well never mind," I said, "Someone wants to give you a drink." I was just about to say that I did not have a description when I said "Ginger always was on time." "Well, I never did," she retorted, "That's my old milkman—he was never late and he used to say everyday two pints of your old milk stout." "Ah," I said, "Even the milkman comes back," as the congregation laughed.

I left her with that comment and turned my attention to a gentleman who was sitting half way along the back row. "You sir," I said, as he realised I was speaking to him, "There is a very attractive lady who wishes to show herself to you." He didn't answer so I continued, "She was young when she died—only about forty-five. She must have been very close for she brings you such love. I would say she passed over about two or three years ago. Helen, yes," I confirmed her name. "It was Helen," I repeated.

Up until that moment the man had not spoken—he just sat there open-mouthed until the silence was broken by a lady who was sitting next to him. "She's got a nerve," I heard. "I beg your pardon," I said, as my ears couldn't believe what I was hearing. "That was his fancy piece," she continued, oblivious of the listening audience. The man shifted uncomfortably on his seat. "Oh, I knew he was carrying on all right. It all came out at the funeral. Well you can tell her from me that she can jolly well leave us alone." The packed hall tittered on hearing this rather delicate bit of scandal that I had just unravelled. "Yes, well," I said, feeling embarrassed, "The Spirit world is of love," and thereby hoped that the remark would help the situation.

However, it only heaped more coal on the already smouldering fire, for as I prepared to go to my next recipient, the lady decided that now was a good time as any to have an argument with her thoroughly unhappy partner. After a good deal of commotion the couple were escorted from the hall. On their departure the hall filled with good-natured laughter. Fortunately, the rest of the evening went well with no more mishaps. We finished the evening, as we had begun, by singing loudly to the last hymn.

"I don't believe it," I said irritably, as I returned to the office the following day. "Just one day's leave, that's all I've had and just look at the work piled on my desk." There were papers everywhere. "Never mind," said my colleague who shared the office with me,

"It proves one thing—that you're missed." I grimaced as I settled down to concentrate on my workload. So busy was I that on looking at my watch I was amazed to see that I had worked well into my lunch period.

I cleared a space for my sandwiches. The office was empty and I enjoyed the peace and quiet as I munched my marmite sandwiches and drank my coffee. I settled back on my chair and closed my eyes as I thought about the forthcoming evening's event. I wonder what we will find at this haunted house. It seemed strange that I was always scared whenever I had to face this sort of problem. But I knew, no matter how I felt, that if I was needed I could not turn my back. I sighed. Bill was right. We didn't seem to have any time to ourselves anymore. Gone were the days of spending evenings quietly watching television. Still at least we didn't have the time to get bored. I smiled as I remembered Bill's remark that he never had me to himself. No wonder we make such a good team together, I thought, sharing our lives with others. One thing—there was never time to have disagreements.

I finished my lunch and turned my attention to the more pressing things of the day and thought no more of the evening's adventure until preparing our evening meal. The potatoes were boiling away merrily on the cooker, sending the lid of the saucepan noisily up and down. The two large pork chops spat out at me angrily and the hot fat made me jump as it hit my arm. Bill came running into the kitchen as I cried out. "Are you O.K.?" he asked, as he watched me running cold water over my arm. "I think so," I replied, "Those stupid chops decided to pick an argument with me and it looks as if they have won." Ugly red marks rapidly appeared on my wrist. "You should take more care," said Bill, as he gave me a kiss, "Had a good day?" "No," I replied, "A really awful day." "Sorry," he said, in a playful voice, "You shouldn't go taking days off." With that remark I chased him out of the kitchen.

We were both ready in good time. We had enjoyed our meal and had discussed the day's events and put the world to rights. We both liked this part of the day best. Bill left the house before me to start the car and I checked that I had the address of our evening's adventure. I really must turn out my handbag sometime, I thought, the junk I carry about is disgusting. I always had a feeling of guilt when looking for something, but this was only momentary. My bag contained all sorts of interesting things—it reminded one of a white elephant stall—never too sure of what you might find. I found the address and we sat for a few moments whilst Bill checked the A to Z.

I settled myself comfortably in my seat and let my whole body relax from the traumas of the day. I was also preparing myself for possible psychic powers which may be required of me. By the time we reached the house I felt able to cope with anything that came my way.

We were about ten minutes late reaching the house as we had got lost a couple of times en route. No sooner had I put my hand on the door knocker when the door opened, making me jump out of my skin. A tall, thin man stood at the door. He was dressed in a pair of grey flannel trousers, which were very creased at the knees, and an off-white shirt, which looked as scruffy as his trousers—I am sure neither article had ever seen an iron. After he had made sure we were his expected guests, he escorted us into a small untidy-looking room.

The house was one of the old-type council houses and the first thing I noticed was the ugly pipes which were exposed all round the room—about one foot away from the ceiling. At some time they had been painted the same colour as the distemper on the walls—a weak blue—and by the look of things another coat of paint over the whole room wouldn't have gone amiss. The impression given was one of gloom and I wanted out immediately. To say I felt uncomfortable was putting it mildly.

"Do sit down," said the man, "I'll tell the wife you have arrived." We both sat down on the settee. I didn't dare look at Bill for fear of him saying something and being overheard. I could tell that he was feeling just as uncomfortable as I in this awful room. A large black and white television set stood in one corner and it had been left on—blaring out some dreadful music, which didn't help the situation. Even if Bill and I had wanted to speak to one another it would have been difficult.

My thoughts were interrupted as a woman of about forty entered the room. "Good evening," she said, "How nice of you to come," speaking loudly in order to be heard over the racket coming from the television. "You found us all right then?" "Yes, thank you," I replied.

I studied the lady carefully as she stood uncertainly in the middle of the room, obviously nervous in our presence. She kept rubbing her hands together and by the way she kept turning her head towards the door seemed to be expecting someone else to enter.

"Do you mind if we turn the television off?" I said, beginning to get very agitated. "Oh, yes, I'm sorry," she said, switching off the offending apparatus. It left a wonderful silence. "I leave it on," the woman explained, "So that they won't hear me—otherwise they never give me any peace." She spoke in a hushed voice. The television cracked as the set began to cool down. "Hear that," she said, "It's listening to us. I've got guests," she said crossly, as she looked towards the set. My husband smiled kindly at her and told her that it was only the set cooling down. "Oh, no," she replied, "It's Jim. He hides inside, but now you are here that will stop him. They are going to catch you," she said, wagging her finger at the tube.

I was just about to tell her that it was all in her imagination when the man who had opened the door to us came into the room. "Alf, tell them about Jim," said the woman, "Doesn't he spy on us?" "Yes, my wife is right—if you sit quiet you will hear him." I turned to Bill perplexed by the whole affair. How on earth are we going to get through to them both, I wondered.

Suddenly the pipes around the wall began to gurgle and bang. "O.K. Jim, we hear you." This time it was the man who spoke, "What do you think?" he said, turning to us, "Can you stop him, only he is slowly driving us mad? Since we've moved to this house he has been causing us trouble. Hasn't he darling?" As he spoke his voice began to rise excitedly. "We've called in all sorts of people, but nothing has been any good—it's because they won't believe us." "That's right," interrupted his wife, "We have even had a priest in, but he seemed in too much of a hurry to get back to his church rather than help us."

The pipes started up again as the back boiler heated up. "See what we have to put up with—he doesn't stop," said the lady, as she looked up at the pipes. I, for once, was lost for words. I turned to Bill in the hope that he might be able to bring some sanity to the situation. These people seemed to be completely out of their minds—and they certainly didn't require the services of a medium—more like a head doctor.

My husband stood up, and as he caught my eye he winked. He addressed the couple in a gentle but firm voice. "How do you know his name is Jim—did he tell you?" "He didn't need to—it's the wife's brother." I watched quite fascinated as the man spoke. "You see we always had problems with her side of the family—they tried to stop our marriage. Her brother Jim was a heavy drinker—drunk himself to death in the finish. He did, didn't he Nelly?"

His wife nodded, but interrupted her husband by continuing the story. "We ran away to get married. My brother said then if he died first he would haunt us." At that moment the pipes gave a resounding bang as if to answer her. She threw her arms around my husband's neck as if seeking protection—at the same time calling her brother's name telling him to go away.

The look on Bill's face was one of alarm and embarrassment. With great difficulty he broke loose from what seemed a demented woman's grasp. In a controlled steady voice, which deserved an Oscar, my husband began to explain the rudiments of the cooling hot water pipes and television sets. I listened to his explanation, marvelling at his natural deliverance—as if this sort of antic happened all the time.

Alf and Nelly were not going to accept a simple solution. They both shook their heads simultanously. "It's all right," said Alf, "Don't try and hide it from us, we know it's Jim, and so do you," he said, turning towards me so that his eyes were staring directly into mine. I blinked, trying to think of an acceptable and feasible answer to their problem.

Suddenly, inspiration hit me. Why not, I answered myself, as the thought began to grow. I faced them squarely. I said, "Would you like me to speak to Jim for you? I could if you wish." From the corner of my eye I saw Bill's astonished face, unable to believe that I could possibly have been taken in by the story. The odd couple looked back at me—relief showing on their faces.

"Would you?" Nelly said, "I would be ever so grateful." "Of course," I replied, "No trouble at all." By this time my husband was standing open-mouthed as I, in a matter of fact attitude, prepared myself for what would seemingly look like a proposed psychic sitting.

"If you will both sit over there," I pointed to the vacant chairs across the room, "And Bill, if you will sit next to me." I patted the seat at my side, and gave him a wink so that he knew everything was under control. "I will try and contact Jim." Bill obediently sat down next to me and I closed my eyes.

After a short while I started to take large over-emphasised breaths. I must admit my performance was pretty good for I knew that our two freinds were enthralled by the whole procedure. After a few minutes I called out in a loud voice, "Jim, Jim, are you there?" The room was devoid of any noise. Please, I prayed, let the pipes knock now. "Jim," I repeated, "Can you hear me?" I would have loved at that moment to have taken a peep at Bill, but knew that I had to put up the performance of my life in order to help the tormented minds of these two people.

"Jim," I called again, majestically. This time, with a loud bang, the pipes answered on cue. "Thank you for coming," I said, "But can you tell me why you are trying to upset these good people?" At this point I pretended to be listening. "Oh, I see. I am sure Nelly will be only too happy to help." "What does he want?" I heard Nelly whisper. I directed my voice to where they were sitting. "Jim doesn't wish you any harm, he is just lonely. All he wants is a loving home. Will you help him—he wants to stay with you both?" "Why, of course he can stay," they answered together, "As long as you want, Jim." "Thank you," I cried out to them, "Jim is so happy now," and as if to join in with the charade, the pipes yet again played their noisy tune.

I took a few more deep breaths and then slowly opened my eyes. "Well," I said, looking at them, not daring to look at my husband, "The condition in this room seems to be so much lighter now. Can you feel it?" "Certainly," replied Bill enthusiastically.

"Well, would you believe it," said Alf as he stood up, "Fancy old Jim only wanting to be with us." "It is amazing," I answered, as I put on my coat, "But Spirit are often accused of being what they are not. Still," I continued, "I shouldn't think you will have any more trouble now. Jim won't harm you and you know now that he only wants to share your life." Bang, bang, went the blessed pipes. "O.K.," Nelly laughed, "I hear you." Then we all laughed as the gurgles went again.

When at last we were in the privacy of our own car Bill held my head in his hands and said, "You, my darling, are a perfect actress." Maybe, but it saved the day. We started to giggle about the experience we had just been through. Our laughter relieved the tensions that had built up and we felt exhausted from the humour of the situation, which of course, could have been an unpleasant and frightening haunting.